How to Start Run & Grow a Successful

Pet Hotel Business

Dog Boarding, Cat Boarding, Pet Kennel, Doggie Daycare & Pet Sitting

Make Money Be Your Own Boss, Work with Animals You Love & Adore

By

Rebecca Floyd

Copyrighted Material

Copyright © 2021 – CSB Academy Publishing Company

All Rights Reserved.

Without limiting the rights under the copyright laws, no part of this publication may be reproduced, stored in or introduced into a retrieval system, or transmitted, in any form or by any means (electronic, mechanical, photocopying, recording or otherwise), without the prior written consent of the publisher of this book.

CSB Academy Publishing Company publishes its books and guides in a variety of electronic and print formats, Some content that appears in print may not be available in electronic format, and vice versa.

CSB Academy Publishing Co.

Cover Design

By

Stephanie Martin

First Edition

Contents

About the Author *15*

Starting a Pet Hotel – Introduction *18*

Typical Day at a Pet Boarding Hotel *21*

    Potential Profit 22

    Location 23

    Initial Investment 23

    Independent Business vs. Franchising 24

    Is It Right for You? 24

    Skills, Experience, and Knowledge Needed 25

        Knowledge 26

        Experience 26

        Skills 26

What to Consider Before Starting *28*

    The Paperwork 30

        Industry Summary 30

        Industry Trends 31

    Crafting a Business Plan 32

        Executive Summary 34

        Business Description 36

- Marketing 37
- Target Audience 38
- Competition 39
- Promotional Strategy 40
- Sales Projections 41
- Seasonality 42
- Pricing 43
- Management and Operations 45
- Financial Projections 46
- Appendix 49

Naming Your Business 51
- What Will You Offer 52
- Where You're Located 52
- Avoid Words that are Hard to Pronounce, Spell, or Hear 53
- Alliterations and Rhyming Words 54
- Avoid Initials or Obscure Acronyms 54
- Imagery Words 55
- Consider the Owner's Name 55
- Consider the Name of the Competition 55
- Trademark Search 56
- Local Search 56
- State Entity Search 57
- Domain Availability 58

    Social Media Profiles 58

Specific Startup Costs *60*

Finding Financing 62

    Personal Assets 62

    Bank Loans 62

    Revolving Loan Funds 64

    Online Lenders 64

    Home Equity 65

    Peer to Peer Lending 65

    Credit Cards 66

    Retirement Accounts 66

    Customer Financing 67

    Angel Investors 68

Form a Legal Entity *69*

Sole Proprietorship 70

    Partnership 70

    Limited Liability Company (LLC) 72

    Corporation 73

Register for Taxes 75

Bank Account and Credit Card 77

    Open a Bank Account 78

    Get a Credit Card 78

Permits and Licenses 78
    What is a Business License? 79
    Occupancy Permits 80
    Occupational or Professional Licensing 80
    Sales Tax Permits 80
    Resale Certificate 81
    Unemployment and Workers' Compensation Registration 81

Insurance 81
    Challenges Facing the Pet Industry 82
    Client and Pet Safety 82
    Staff Safety 83
    Loss of Business 83
    Animal Floater/Bailee 84
    Lost Key 84
    Commercial Liability 84
    Worker's Compensation 85
    Business Interruption 85

Operating Considerations *86*

    Expenses 86
    Regulations 87
    Permits and Zoning 87
    Space 88

Construction Requirements 88

Sanitary Conditions 89

Segregation 89

Mitigating Liabilities 90

    Keep All Areas Locked 90

    Security Systems 90

    Staff Training 91

    Cleaning Products 91

    Non-Refundable Deposit 91

    Company Policy 92

    Signed Policy Sheet 92

    Confirm Pet Information 92

Pricing 93

    Calculate Fixed Costs 94

    Estimate Variable Costs 95

    Combine Costs 95

    Pricing Model 96

    Pricing Special Services 97

    Determining What to Charge 99

Amenities to Offer 100

    24/7 Staffing 100

    Play Areas 101

    Boarding Other Pets 101

Building Your Facility *102*

Choosing a Location 102
Buying vs. Leasing 105
Looking for a Property... 106
Equipment.. 107
The Construction Process 109
Choosing a Building 109
Environmental Studies 111
Mechanical Systems...111
Roofing System 112
Thermal Insulation 113
Acoustical Components 113
Americans with Disabilities Act (ADA) Compliance 114
Drainage and Slab Work..115
Life Safety..116
Things to Consider Before Construction 116
Common Project Delivery Methods 118
Selecting and Qualifying the Contractor and Design Team 124
Preparing for the Construction Process............. 126
Functionality 127

Durability 127

Building Layout 128

Cleaning 130

Feeding 130

Outdoor Access 131

Check-In and Out 131

Flooring 132

Focus on Cats *139*

Why Board Cats 139

Clients Who Board Cats 140

Designs for Cats 142

Outside the Condo Considerations 144

Drainage Issues 145

Ceiling Considerations 145

Air Quality 146

Consider a Screened Porch 147

Important Components 147

Clean Spaces 147

Odor Elimination 148

Comfort 149

Activities and Distractions 150

Helpful Software *152*

Client and Pet Management 153

Customer Portal and Online Booking 153

Reservation Management Features 154

Key Communication Features 154

Retail Features 154

Marketing Features 155

Staff Management Features 155

Suggested Software 156

Marketing Your Business..157

Target Market 157

Define Your Brand 158

How to Focus Your Marketing 158

Examine Financial Reports 160

The Strategy Session 162

Marketing Options 165

Building an Online Presence 165

    Create a Website 166

    Create a Social Media Presence 166

    Local SEO Optimization 167

Develop a Referral System 168

Asking for Reviews 168

Learning How to Ask 169

Become Creative 169

Learn from What Doesn't Work 169

Paid Advertising and Facebook Ads 170

Google Advertising 171

Retargeting to Improve Traffic 172

How to Use Marketing in the Slow Seasons 172

Fun in the Off-Season 173

Themed Parties 174

Dress Up Nights 175

Pet and People Mixers 175

Spa and Grooming Services 175

Sporting Events for Competitive Pets 176

Use the Internet 177

Expand Beyond On-Site Services 178

Ensure You're Making a Profit 178

How to Use Your Website for Marketing 179

Own Your Web Address 179

Display Professional Association Logos 180

Check Your Web Design Standards 180

Easy Phone Number 181

Review Your Website 181

Include a Business Logo 182

Add Photos 182

Professional Association Content 182

Remove Irrelevant Information 183

Highlight Seasonal Services 183

Improving Your Web Presence 184

Shorten Home Page Content 184

Add Photos and Videos 185

Don't Divert, Convert 185

Google Places 185

Web Analytics 186

Online Reviews 187

Bold Design Change 187

How to Use Facebook for Marketing 188

Tour the Facility 190

Introduce Staff Members 190

Offer a Q&A Session 191

Introduce Pets 191

Go Behind the Scenes 191

Highlight Accomplishments 192

Recommend Other Businesses 192

Review Top Toys 192

Offer Pet Care Tips 193

Introducing Satisfied Clients 193

How to Use Retention Marketing to Keep Clients 194

Benefits of Retention Marketing 195

Stay in Touch 196

Education 197

Say Thank You 197

Be Social 198

Daily Operational Considerations 199

Health and Safety 200

How Design Helps 200

Creating a Health and Safety Program 201

Having an Emergency Preparedness Plan 209

Defining an Emergency 210

Talk with Your Insurance Agent 212

Internal Resources 212

Outside Help 213

Staff Training 214

Review the Facility and Grounds 215

Emergency Response Elements 216

Evacuation Procedures and Operational Shut Down 217

Protecting Vital Records 218

Restoring Operations and Assessing Damage 219

Implementation 219

Hiring Employees **221**

Hiring Your First Employee 221

Training Employees 222

The Real Cost of an Employee 224

Employer Responsibilities 225

Determining Staffing Needs 226

Retaining Good Employees 228

Effective Daily Management **229**

Streamline Your Business 229

Set up Processes 230

Track Expenses 230

Use the Right Software 230

Hire When Needed 231

Invest in Business Growth 231

Utilize Effective Marketing Strategies 231

Automate What You Can 232

Partner with Similar Services 232

Expand Services 232

Measure Everything 233

Conclusion *234*

About the Author

I have been in the pet care industry for over a decade. I first started working as a receptionist in my uncle's veterinary clinic at age 18. I had owned dogs and cats in my childhood, but never thought about making it a career.

When I was thinking about college, I realized that becoming a vet technician was a viable option. When my uncle retired and sold his practice, I worked as a tech for the new vet for a few years. We found ourselves receiving frequent requests to board animals on a short-term basis. Usually, these requests came from pet owners who were our regular vet clients going out of town for a few days. We took these dogs and cats in for mostly weekends and holidays. I realized that in my area, quality pet boarding was essential.

I started my own pet boarding business out of an old daycare building. The daycare had been closed down for a while, but it had easily convertible facilities for pet boarding. The building had a nearly commercial-sized kitchen and 4 different classrooms, each with its own attached bathroom. It also had a large fenced-in yard that used to include playground equipment and a big indoor community space, presumably for assemblies or indoor playtime. A building originally built to house children during the day was easily converted to house cats and dogs.

My pet boarding business was born on a shoestring budget. In my book, I will show you how to start your own pet hotel from the ground up. This book draws on my personal experiences and research I conducted years ago.

I hope this book helps you achieve your dreams. Would you kindly consider leaving a review on the platform where you purchased this book? Online reviews can help me reach a wider audience. Thank you in advance!

* * *

I must give special thanks to my friend Yvette White. Without her guidance and constant support, this book would not have been possible. Thank you!

STARTING A PET HOTEL – INTRODUCTION

A pet hotel is an upscale boarding facility that caters to the needs of clients' pets for any length of time. The pet industry has been booming in recent years, and many busy pet owners need to find care for their pets when they aren't home. Starting your own pet hotel can allow you to build a profitable business while helping to provide a need for pet owners.

While this may sound like the ideal business venture, it is

important to ensure you understand everything involved in starting and running a pet hotel before taking the leap. So first, we're going to look at what it takes to start and run a pet hotel; then we'll look at the process for starting one; and lastly, we'll consider what you need to do to run one. At the end of this book, if you're still ready, then you'll be completely prepared to start your own pet hotel.

The traditional pet kennel is designed to house and care for animals. These facilities are often indoor with built-in dog runs, while some are indoor/outdoor with a large, fenced area. Occasionally, a facility will be attached to a veterinary practice in case there is a medical emergency. Sleeping areas are often private in order to provide safety and security overnight.

Private kennels will often house fewer animals. Zoning and permit laws will influence what a private kennel looks like, but in general, they are on at least five acres of land and house no more than ten animals at a time. These are often the best choice for owners of animals that are socially anxious or have special needs requiring one-on-one attention.

Luxury kennels or hotels are ones with all the high-end amenities. This could include things like heated swimming pools, custom furnishings, massages, and fresh-baked treats. These hotels also typically have more on-site staff than other general kennels, so the animals can have individual attention.

TYPICAL DAY AT A PET BOARDING HOTEL

Most clients typically envision a job where you get to sit around and play with puppies all day. The truth is, when you own a pet hotel, there is a great deal of work to be done throughout the day. Some of the activities that you may be required to do when running a pet hotel are the following:

Checking customers into and out of the facility

Cleaning hotel rooms and any play areas

Feeding pets and medicating as needed

Exercising animals

Administrative tasks, including answering emails and phone calls, taking reservations, and paying bills

Keeping up with marketing and advertising efforts

Many pet hotels also offer additional services, such as grooming. Before starting your pet hotel, it is important to determine which services you will offer and ensure you are properly equipped and staffed to meet those needs. We'll look a little closer at this later. For now, let's consider what your potential profit can be from starting a pet hotel.

POTENTIAL PROFIT

There are several factors that can influence the profits

you earn from starting a pet hotel. Experienced professionals starting with a franchise hotel can easily earn millions in annual profit. A smaller operation in the right location can easily earn between $32,000 and $48,000 within the first year. Let's consider a few of the factors that can influence profit.

LOCATION

The location of your business and your nearby competitors is a big factor. For example, a business in a small town with few pet owners may have a lower income than a pet hotel in a community with many dog owners.

INITIAL INVESTMENT

The amount you invest in starting your business can also affect how much profit you earn. The less you are able to invest, the more profit you'll get once your business starts operations.

INDEPENDENT BUSINESS VS. FRANCHISING

In general, operating a franchise pet hotel will offer you greater earning potential than starting an independent business. This is because the initial investment for a franchise is often lower, and you benefit from a recognized brand name, corporate resources, and support. Even individual franchises can have a major difference in potential profits.

The best way to ensure profitability if you are starting an independent pet hotel is to consider the community's needs and offer services that meet them. Also looking for additional ways to increase profits, such as offering treats, toys, grooming services, and other amenities. We'll consider a lot of these areas in greater detail later. But first, let's finish our introduction by considering if starting a pet hotel is right for you.

IS IT RIGHT FOR YOU?

Pet hotels focus on caring for and pampering pets when

their owners are unable to do so. Therefore, the most important requirement for pet hotel owners is being an animal lover or pet owner. This will help you identify with your customers and interact more closely with the pets. You should also have some experience running a small business, managing schedules, and handling numerous customer accounts.

Those who are compassionate and have a strong business mind are often the ones who will have the most success in starting a pet hotel business. Consider some of the skills, experience, and knowledge that will help you when starting a pet hotel business.

Skills, Experience, and Knowledge Needed

You don't need a business degree in order to start a pet hotel. However, there are some skills and experiences that can help improve your chances of starting and running a successful business. Let's consider these.

KNOWLEDGE

It is important to have some knowledge of general pet care. Do you know how to care for each type of pet you'll be accommodating? Experience handling pets is important for providing better, safer care for everyone, including the animal, the owner, and the staff.

EXPERIENCE

Some experience with pet first aid and medical care is also important. While being boarded, an illness or injury requiring treatment may arise, and handling these situations appropriately is important. Formal pet CPR or first aid training and certification can help.

SKILLS

It is also important to have customer service skills. This is an area where you can help your business stand out and build customer loyalty. This is often done through the following areas.

Attention to detail is important because it helps in every aspect of the business, from administering medications to monitoring a pet's normal behavior. As a business owner, you need to be involved in all aspects of the business.

You'll also need some management experience. As your hotel grows, you'll need to hire additional staff to assist. You'll need to be able to hire, train and manage your employees.

What to Consider Before Starting

Pet owners are often anxious about the safety and care of their pets. Be prepared to receive many unusual requests that often exceed your typical standard of care. Make sure you are prepared by having policies in place for these extra requests, so you can fulfill any requests you honor.

Good policies are key to keeping your business running smoothly. Before you first start a pet hotel, you need to consider your vaccine and health requirements for boarding pets and outline them in writing. This is also a good time to have a policy outlining what you will do if a pet experiences a medical emergency and to develop relationships with local veterinarians who want to work with you.

When you run a pet hotel, you'll often have to work the holidays, as these are often when your facility is going to be at full capacity. While owning a pet hotel can be profitable, many facilities also offer additional services to increase profits. Some upselling opportunities that are convenient for pet owners include things like nail trims, grooming, and training.

You can also offer amenities such as extra playtime sessions, special treats, and organic products. While all of these amenities may be tempting, it is best to keep things small and manageable when you first start and then branch out as you see what most appeals to your audience.

However, the first part you need to focus on before getting started with a pet hotel is the paperwork. A lot of work goes into preparing a facility before you even get to the physical part of building your business. So, let's go into detail on the paperwork you need to get your business established.

The Paperwork

When it comes to establishing the paperwork for your pet hotel business, the first thing you need to do is establish an understanding of the industry. To do this, you need to consider the industry as a whole, as well as the specifics that can impact your pet hotel.

Industry Summary

According to statistics, the 2014 to 2019 period was one of significant growth for the pet boarding industry. Within these five years, there was a 6.2 percent growth, and the number of pet boarding businesses increased to 123,900. Employment also increased to 218,674, and the projected revenue as of 2019 was $9 billion.

Part of this growth was due to an increase in the number of pet owners in the United States. From 2017 to 2018, 38.4 percent of households owned dogs, while 25.4 percent of households owned cats. This means over 48,000,000 households had dogs, and over 31,000,000 had cats. With pet ownership so popular, the need for services such as pet boarding has increased. There was also an increase in per capita disposable income from 2014 to 2019, meaning more people have additional money to spend on luxuries such as vacations, which increases the need for pet boarding.

INDUSTRY TRENDS

There are plenty of trends shaping the pet boarding industry. Pet owners are increasingly tech-savvy, so most boarding businesses need to focus on technology. This can be done by offering online reservations or by having video cameras that stream to a website so pet owners can see their pets no matter where they travel. Small details like this can help your business appeal to pet owners and set you apart from the competition.

The industry can also benefit from premium offerings that provide owners with unique, desirable services. Luxuries like extra-large kennels, furnishings that offer the comfort of a home, and indulgences like treats and toys can make a pet's stay at your hotel more enjoyable. These premium offerings also give you the chance to upsell and increase business profits. They can also help increase customer loyalty and encourage repeat business. Knowing these trends and industry summary can help you when you prepare the most important document to get started with your business: the business plan.

Crafting a Business Plan

Now that you have the idea to start a pet hotel, the next step you need to take in order to start your business is to write up a business plan. Not only is this document needed to approach a bank, but studies have also shown that a business plan increases the chances of your business being successful.

The business plan should outline building costs, zoning fees, permits, design fees, materials, advertising, and licensing, among other things. When you write a business plan, you need to make sure that the area around you isn't saturated with similar businesses and that your business will be supported by the community. Let's look at the details of writing a business plan.

Writing a business plan may be overwhelming at first, but breaking it down into manageable sections makes it a little easier. To get started, you should first write about the opportunity, product, and services you plan to offer. Then you can work your way to the more difficult areas, such as marketing, operations, and financials. Also, keep in mind that the first draft of your business plan doesn't need to be perfect; it just needs to get the concepts onto paper, and you can make refinements later. If you find yourself stuck on a section, you can also come back later with more details.

It is also important that you tailor your business plan to your intended audience. For example, a business plan focused on a bank loan will be less focused on exit strategy and return on investment than a plan for equity investors. Also, a business plan written for internal use will look different from a business plan for financing, as a bank isn't going to be as interested in a business's detailed day-to-day operations.

While there isn't a specific format a business follows,

there are some generally accepted guidelines that people use, so the subjects don't flow in random order. The Business Description section of the plan focuses on painting a picture of the business and its success. The Marketing and Management part is where your research and business strategy are developed.

Lastly, the Financial Projections part focuses on the numbers that you use in the business plan. In addition, a business plan should include a title page, table of contents, and an appendix to further organize the document. In addition, the length of a business plan is as long as it needs to be. The more complex or sophisticated a business, the longer the plan. Most business plan narratives are four to ten pages, plus the financials and appendix pages.

EXECUTIVE SUMMARY

This is the first part of the business plan, but is often the last to be written. This section offers the reader a quick overview of what the proposal is about and what the plan asks for. This part is important for lenders, as they often scan this section and make a quick decision on whether the project is something they can lend to.

The executive summary is often about half a page in length and includes the same information you would have in an elevator pitch, including the following:

- A short version of the business concept

- Service proposition and/or product description

- Trends in the industry

- Customer demographics

- Details of the management team

- Potential start date

- Equity position of the owner

- How much funds are requested, and how it will be used

The key to an executive summary is concision. You'll include more details later in the other sections of the business plan.

BUSINESS DESCRIPTION

The focus of this section is to objectively describe and justify your business concept. This area typically includes:

- Mission statement

- What the business will do

- Description of services provided and/or products offered

- Trends and information for the industry

- Detailed business structure

- The status of the business

- The current and future goals

You should note any facts or figures along with their sources. This information is important for backing up any assumptions you make in the business plan. Think of this section as the one that helps paint a picture of the business's potential, along with the facts explaining why the business will succeed. You should convey some energy and excitement in this section so the reader becomes enthusiastic about your business and why it will be a success.

After you describe what your business will do, you'll also want to describe any services and products you're going to offer. It is important to show why the services or products you offer are better than the competition, although this will be covered later. If you can't answer this, then you may want to consider why you are opening your business. Your answer should simply be that you offer a cheaper solution than the competition, because anyone can easily reduce prices. Rather, you need something else that makes your business different from the competition.

MARKETING

This is one of the more important and yet often

overlooked sections of the business plan. No matter how good the quality of your products or services, a business can easily get lost in advertising if it doesn't know who its target customers are. All of this will take you some research. Spend time on this section to get to know your target audience; it will also help you later when developing a marketing and advertising plan.

Target Audience

The first thing you need to do is determine who the core group of people you want to attract is and what common characteristic they share. These characteristics can include age, income, race, religion, education, hobbies, interests, and geographic location. While everyone may need what you have to offer, the main question is how to market to these people in order to get the best return on your investment in advertising.

By determining who is most likely to use your services, you can strategically focus your advertising spending. While you can place ads anywhere to reach an entire geographic area, you need to do so in a way that still makes a profit. You need to advertise with a focus on the groups MOST likely to use your services.

You never want to start a new business without having a marketing plan in place. This will only result in wasted funds that could be better spent elsewhere in your business. This section helps you determine where to allocate your funds and make informed decisions.

Competition

The pet industry is a very competitive marketplace, and no matter how creative your concept is, there will be competition. Trying to run your business more efficiently than the competition will be a challenge as a startup. Rather, you should focus on planning how your business can be different and compete with others in a less direct form.

Ask yourself where you can market differently and if there is a specific niche that isn't being fulfilled. Is there some way that you can add more value to your services? Even if there isn't direct competition in the area, there will still be indirect competition from other types of businesses. For example, while there may not be other hotels in the area, there may still be pet sitting services that offer to go to a client's home to look after their pets. It is important that you always find a competitor and show how you can overcome them. If you indicate that you have no competition in the plan, it will be viewed as either a lack of market for what you are offering or as insufficient research.

For this area, you should evaluate at least 3 and no more than 5 direct competitors. List information about who they are, how long they've been in operation, where they are located, what services they offer, their perception of pricing, quality of services, and more. Then compare the advantages and disadvantages with your business. Take your time to research and gather all the necessary details.

PROMOTIONAL STRATEGY

Once you've completed the research for the above steps, the promotional strategy portion should be fairly easy. Knowing your target audience, research the types of media and marketing you'll need. While there likely won't be a single best way, knowing your target audience is the first step in finding the best possible ways. You'll also likely need to refine the promotional strategy over time.

When you develop a promotional strategy, it is important to remember that advertising isn't cheap and can sometimes be difficult to tell whether it is working. Any method you use to track advertising will provide data on whether a marketing channel is worth investing more in or should be discontinued.

SALES PROJECTIONS

This is one of the more challenging parts of the business plan. This number is likely going to turn out wrong, but that's to be expected. What matters is that the figures are supported by reasonable, justifiable data. Simply taking a number and saying you'll make that in a year won't work. Rather, you should use a variety of sources to come up with a viable number, such as the following:

    Industry journals

    Trade groups

Industry experts

Average household spending

Census data

Even if this number is not likely to be right, it is still important to do the research. When preparing the financial projections later in the business plan, this number will help you to determine the feasibility of the business. The comfort of the entrepreneurs with this percentage is going to vary based on the competition, industry, and other factors, but it is a starting point to confirm whether or not the business is worth investing in.

SEASONALITY

In some businesses, this can be more significant than in others. Either way, it is important to estimate, as it will indicate whether additional investment may be needed at some point. Is your business likely to experience peaks and lows? Estimating seasonality will tell you whether enough revenue will be generated in the good months to keep the business going for the rest of the year. When you start a new business, cash is critical, and investors don't want to see a business start underfunded, because that means it may fail before it gets a chance to succeed. The business plan will provide this information and indicate whether better planning is needed for a successful business.

To determine seasonality, estimate the percentage of sales for each month. These percentages will eventually be used in the cash flow statement. You can get some estimates from sources such as industry associations, forums, business owners, and others. Negative numbers in the cash flow statement of the financial projections are an indication of the need for additional investment.

PRICING

Pricing will have a major impact on how a service and/or product is perceived in the market. Prices too low compared to the competition will give off the perception of being cheap and unreliable. Prices that are too high relative to the competition, without a premium feature or other benefit, will likely lead to fewer customers. Pricing is a very complex issue that we'll discuss more closely later, but there are a few things you want to keep in mind when it comes to this section of your business plan.

Basing your pricing on the competition isn't always the best method. A competitor may have operated for many years and can operate at a lower cost since they have paid off equipment. The other side of that is that new equipment offers more benefits that people are willing to pay for. You should also be aware that you don't think a competitor is making money simply because they offer a lower price; they may not be making as much as you think.

It is common for a new business to want to start with a lower cost in order to get started. It can be better to promote at full price and offer discounts until the business becomes better known. This is because it can be difficult to raise prices once a customer is used to the lower prices.

Sometimes an entrepreneur has a hard time valuing their time appropriately. Make sure you price your time doing work when you evaluate expenses. If you plan to expand your business, you need to establish processes so others can do the work. If you don't factor pricing as an expense for others to do the work, then you may not have the option to expand.

Pricing is often the easiest part of marketing to change. Businesses don't operate in a vacuum, and your competitors may lower their prices once a new business opens in order to make the new business shut down before they get a foothold. This is yet another reason why you want to be different from the competition.

While it can be difficult to deal with pricing, you shouldn't be afraid to charge more for a service or product, especially if you are going to be offering something better than the competition. Just make sure you have enough customers who want your premium pet hotel offering before you get started.

MANAGEMENT AND OPERATIONS

This section is for you to describe who is going to manage the business and fill the necessary positions to deliver the service and/or products. Initially, these may all be the entrepreneur, but there may be a need to hire additional staff in the future.

If you are seeking funding, you should include bios and resumes for all key individuals and owners of the business. The resumes should be included in the appendix. Showcase the people's experience and education and how they enable the business to operate successfully. Lenders place a lot of weight on the management team's experience when evaluating a business loan, since this often correlates with a successful business. Some things you want to include in this section are the following:

What positions will need to be filled

When these positions will have to be filled

How much each position will be paid

FINANCIAL PROJECTIONS

The end of the business plan will contain financial projections. These are placed just before the appendix. These are critical pieces of the plan and one of the biggest areas that new businesses struggle with. There is some software that can help you generate these numbers.

There are three main financial statements that a lender is going to want to see:

> Cash flow statement

> Profit and loss statement

> Balance sheet

The information you previously provided in the narrative section must match these financial projections.

The projected cash flow statement is one of the key pieces of the business plan. Like a checkbook register, it will show a schedule of the money that comes into a business and the expenses that need to be paid. This will show whether there is enough cash to sustain the business based on assumptions made. Every part of the business plan is key, but none will matter if cash runs out before the business can turn a profit. If this number turns out to be negative, then the sales need to be increased, expenses reduced, or more cash is needed to get started.

The profit and loss statement is similar to the cash flow statement. It is displayed annually and looks at the after-tax view of the business's financial results.

Lastly, the balance sheet is a summary of an organization's assets, liabilities, and equity at the close of each year. This is often described as a "snapshot" of a company's financial condition and shows a business's value over time.

The initial expenses list all costs prior to opening or expanding a business. You should have quotes available in the appendix for all items costing over $500. There should also be a miscellaneous line item that accounts for about 10% of the total project costs, since there will always be unexpected expenses that aren't planned for. Additional funds may not be needed, but you never want to go back to the bank to ask for more.

You may also need to provide the sources and uses of funds documents. This section would show how the loan money will be used and who is providing it. With a startup business, you'll need to be prepared to use at least 20% of personal money or more, depending on the risk assessment of the business and your level of personal credit.

Lastly, you may need to provide a personal financial statement. If you are seeking bank financing, this statement is required for each person with 20 percent or more ownership. This statement shows each individual's assets.

APPENDIX

The appendix of the business plan is where various pieces of information are placed to back up claims, but it would take up too much room in the narratives. Some things that may be included here are the following:

> Quotes for items that cost over $500

> Resumes from all members of the management team

Research on the industry

Data and trends from demographics

Locational maps, floor plans, blueprints

Contracts and leases

Letters of support

There is a lot that goes into writing a business plan, but it will not only help you get a loan but also make your business stronger. At the very least, it will help you determine what to avoid doing when starting your business. While it may seem easier to have someone else write the plan for you, it is always best to do it yourself if you can. When you write the plan yourself, you will have a better understanding of the business and how you can outline a strategy for success. Once you have a business plan in place, you need to focus on a key area, such as naming your business.

NAMING YOUR BUSINESS

Finding the ideal name for your business can be a challenge. The name not only needs to resonate with your customers but also be available. When you consider the fact that there are over 133,000 dog kennels in the United States, it can be easy to see how finding a unique name can be a challenge.

Choosing the right name for your business will help potential customers understand what services you offer. The name also makes a first impression for your business and helps you stand out from the competition. Let's look at how you can choose the ideal name for your new pet hotel.

The best way to come up with a name for your pet hotel is to brainstorm. As we go through the following tips to name your pet hotel, make a list of words, phrases, and terms that are linked to your business. From there, you will be able to narrow the list and cross off anything you don't like. Once you get down to your top considerations, you need to know how to properly use them. From here, you'll be narrowed down to a final decision and the ideal name for your new pet hotel. So, let's look at some tips to help you get started brainstorming ideas.

What Will You Offer

There are several services a pet hotel can offer aside from standard boarding. So, consider the services you plan to offer when choosing a name. Perhaps you want people to focus more on amenities such as grooming or training. Perhaps there are other specialty services you're offering. Just remember to avoid anything that could limit your business's future growth when choosing a name that reflects the services you offer.

Where You're Located

Many pet hotels are specific to a geographic location. If this is the case, you may want to add a location-specific term to your business name. This can include things like the following:

    Nicknames for your city

Neighborhoods

Regions

States

Descriptive terms

Again, just keep in mind that this will influence the expansion of your business to outside areas. Does the name limit your potential expansion? In this case, it is best to avoid naming your business after the area, should you plan to expand or change the location later.

Avoid Words that are Hard to Pronounce, Spell, or Hear

While many advancements have been made in voice search, many still struggle to understand confusing words or slang. This will limit how easily your business shows up in voice searches. It is also important to avoid complicated words, industry jargon, and the use of numbers in place of letters. Having a unique name is good, but being too unique can be a hindrance. Rather, you want a business name that is simple and easy so potential customers won't have trouble finding you.

ALLITERATIONS AND RHYMING WORDS

These are catchy and help your business name stick. However, they aren't the easiest to come up with. To do this, choose a few of your favorite words from the brainstormed list. Then Google for words that start with the same letter or search for words that rhyme with a word on your list. This is a time-consuming place but it can be a great option if you want to go this route. Make sure you remember to add any exciting results to your brainstorm list. It is important not to overthink any names you come up with. Write down anything you come up with, and you might spark some better ideas later.

AVOID INITIALS OR OBSCURE ACRONYMS

These can be hard to remember and don't make the best business names. They can also be difficult to pronounce and confuse a voice search. Add this to the fact that there are 325 possible two-letter combinations in the English language, and you have a name that is very hard for a customer to remember.

Imagery Words

When brainstorming name ideas, it is also a good idea to consider whether an industry-related word can be used in a logo. This can help to brand your business and reduce marketing investment.

Consider the Owner's Name

If you are still struggling to find a name, consider using the business owner's name. This works well if you plan to stay in the face behind the business. Just keep in mind that if you go this route, it can be more difficult to sell your business in the future, should that be your exit strategy.

Consider the Name of the Competition

Consider the name of your competition. This can help you generate creative ideas while also ensuring you don't choose a name that is too similar to the competition.

Once you have completed these steps, you'll likely have several top choices. The best way to narrow this list is to see which ones are available. This is a vital step in naming your business. If you end up using a name someone else is already using, rebranding your business becomes a costly and time-consuming endeavor. There are several ways to check whether a business name is available for you to use.

Trademark Search

This is the most important one to check. If a name or phrase is trademarked, then you won't be allowed to use it in any similar capacity. Therefore, you should run a trademark search for the name you are considering and cross off any names on the list that aren't available.

Local Search

Just because a name doesn't have a federal trademark doesn't mean the name you want to use is available. There is another type of trademark known as a common law trademark. These aren't filed anywhere, but provide someone who uses the name in commerce with some limited rights within their geographical area to use the name. It is difficult to define how far geographically these rights extend since each industry is different.

However, at a basic level, you shouldn't open a business and name it something similar to a competing business in the same town. If you feel a name could cause confusion among customers, it is best to choose a different name to help you avoid legal issues later.

If you want to do a local search, you can either use a phone book or do a Google search to see if there is any local competition with a similar name to the one you want to use. Cross off any similar names on your list, and keep checking the next option to narrow your potential names.

STATE ENTITY SEARCH

If you plan to register your pet hotel as a corporation or LLC, then you need to register with a unique business name. Each state requires a corporation or LLC to register a unique name for its entity. This doesn't protect your name from being used by someone else, but no one else can register under the same name in your state. If you find a name already in use, cross it off your list and keep searching.

Domain Availability

A website address isn't as critical as the searches above, but it is still worthwhile. Often, you want your domain name to be *yourbusinessname.com* without any confusing numbers, dashes, or special characters. This makes it easier for customers to remember, but they are also difficult to come by. Choosing a name with an available domain name makes it easier for customers to find you online.

Social Media Profiles

Lastly, if you are down to just a few choices, you may want to check whether the names are already in use on social media. Consider which platforms may be important for your marketing and advertising to determine where to start your search. You may need to shorten your name for some social media platforms. Social media is a major factor in advertising these days, so you'll want to make sure you are easy to find on these platforms.

Hopefully, after all this, you will have some good names for your pet hotel. Once you have picked the ideal name for your pet hotel, you can move on to the next step in the process. This is where you need to consider the cost of starting your business.

SPECIFIC STARTUP COSTS

There are plenty of factors that can impact the start-up costs of your pet hotel. Just a few include the location, local laws and regulations, and the size of your business. Keeping these factors in mind, it is recommended that you have a budget of $25,000 to $85,000. The average initial investment will often involve the following:

Land/Location Lease: The average cost is $4,000 per month, and most building owners require a minimum down payment of 2 months.

Facility Build Out: This total cost will depend on the size of the building you are leasing and the features it includes. The average cost is about $45,000.

Business Insurance: Depending on what you need, which we'll discuss later, this can range from $700 to $1,200.

Equipment: This can range from $1,500 to $15,000, depending on the facility size and the services and/or products you plan to offer.

Permits and Deposits: This can range from $1,500 to $7,000.

Website Design: An online presence is key for today's businesses; an in-depth website can cost up to $4,000.

Experienced pet hotel owners suggest having a cash reserve of $15,000 to $25,000. You'll need to determine a specific startup budget that meets your business's needs. Once you have a number in mind, you can start looking into finding appropriate financing.

FINDING FINANCING

Having a good business idea and the necessary skills to run it is one thing, but securing the funding to start your business is another. Funding to start a pet hotel can be difficult to get. To get a loan, the borrower needs to have good credit and be able to personally invest 15-25% of the total start-up costs. Consider the following options you have to help you fund your pet hotel start-up.

PERSONAL ASSETS

These often play a major role in financing a business and are used to borrow against or used as collateral to secure a bank loan. Collateral can include things that you personally own, such as cars, boats, jewelry, stocks, and more. The bank will use the collateral as security for a business loan.

BANK LOANS

These are a popular option for small-business funding, but they can be difficult to obtain. There are a few financing options for bank loans, but the two main ones are conventional and guaranteed.

Conventional loans are made by banks and secured by collateral and the borrower's promise to repay. Banks prefer to make loans for start-up costs tied to hard assets such as buildings, equipment, and vehicles. It can be more difficult to obtain bank funding for working capital expenses such as wages, advertising, and cash flow needs. Banks prefer a borrower with a minimum credit score of 650-680 and full collateral. Borrowers will also need to invest 15-25% of their personal funds in the total project. To apply for these loans, you will need personal tax returns, a business plan, and financial projections.

Guaranteed loans are backed by the federal government through the Small Business Administration (SBA) or, sometimes, the United States Department of Agriculture (USDA). The SBA or USDA is responsible for guaranteeing a percentage of the loan if the business fails and the business owner is unable to repay it. This reduces the bank's risk and can be helpful for those who don't have a sufficient credit score or collateral. The loan guarantee also reduces the amount of personal investment to 10-15%. However, the trade-off with these loans is a longer processing time, higher fees, and higher interest rates.

Revolving Loan Funds

Sometimes known as a microloan, an RLF is a short-term loan for a small amount. These loans often range from $500 to $150,000 and don't have as strict requirements as a bank. These loan programs are available as an economic development tool to help communities improve by financing entrepreneurs who can't obtain capital from banks. These programs are often more focused on job creation than they are on credit scores. These loans are often offered through intermediaries like cities, local economic development agencies, and not-for-profits.

Online Lenders

As the access to funds from traditional banks becomes more difficult for small businesses, alternative lenders are becoming a more popular option. Alternative lenders also offer other benefits, such as less paperwork and an easier application process. There is also greater flexibility in collateral requirements and the types of loans offered. The trade-off is that you'll likely pay more in interest and have shorter terms than you would with a bank, but they do provide a great way to build credit.

Home Equity

Another way to fund a business is to use a home equity loan if you own a home. Home equity loans for a business are often used for a down payment or as collateral to reduce how much money the business owner needs to provide. These are often at a lower interest rate and can be processed faster than a conventional loan.

Peer to Peer Lending

An alternative to borrowing is to consider peer-to-peer lending networks. P2P lending bypasses banks and connects borrowers with investors through internet-based marketplaces. This arrangement serves a need where a bank may not traditionally lend. Often, you can bypass the bank and let people borrow from those who aren't expecting a return. Interest rates are often determined by the credit score of the borrower, but you don't need a great credit score. These lending options provide benefits for both the business and the investor. For businesses, there is quick access to cash and fewer requirements. Investors can diversify their risk across several projects to achieve a better return on investment.

CREDIT CARDS

This can be a quick way to fund a business, and sometimes you can even find 0% financing. While the credit card will be in the business name, the owner's personal credit will still be a major factor in getting the card. Any type of business can get a business card. They are a little riskier than a fixed loan and more expensive after the low introductory rate, but this is still an option for funding. Depending on what you need the funding for, credit cards can be an easier way to finance a business startup or expansion.

RETIREMENT ACCOUNTS

This is often an overlooked source of business funding. Most people don't know they can use their IRA or 401 (k) to start a business, but they also don't have to pay taxes or penalties on the money. This can be a great way to start a business without causing extra debt.

There are two ways to use retirement funds, and it is best to use an established firm, since there can be significant risk if you do it wrong. There are several rules and regulations that apply when using retirement funds from an IRA, and the IRS wants to make sure you aren't improperly using the funds.

CUSTOMER FINANCING

This is an overlooked yet creative way to secure funds to start a business. If you are close to launching, you can ask customers to pre-order before your service or product is ready to sell. An added benefit of pre-selling is that you can see whether the market really wants the service and/or products you are offering. However, you need to make sure you have a solid plan to deliver on time; otherwise, you'll end up with upset customers, and this can hurt your business.

ANGEL INVESTORS

These are individuals who invest in small business startups. You'll need a solid business plan to convince an angel investor to give you the necessary funds. An angel investor isn't the same as a lender. With this option, as you start to make a profit, you will need to give a part of the profits to the angel investor. The angel investor is a part of your business because of their investment, and they will expect a high rate of return. If you are going to ask an investor for money, you need to make sure you provide them with a clear exit strategy, since they often don't want to be involved in a business for more than five years.

Once you have the funding in place, you can move on to the next step of forming a legal entity.

FORM A LEGAL ENTITY

You will also need to form a legal entity, as this is how a business must be organized to operate. There are four main business entities that you can choose from: sole proprietorship, partnership, corporation, and limited liability company (LLC). Each entity has its own pros and cons regarding liability exposure, costs, and administrative requirements. You need to choose a business structure carefully, since it will affect how much you pay in taxes, how you can raise money, and the paperwork you need to file. Let's look at each structure to help you determine which may be right for you.

SOLE PROPRIETORSHIP

This business entity is easy to form and allows you to maintain complete control of your business. If you conduct business activities but don't register as a business entity, you are considered a sole proprietorship. With a sole proprietorship, you don't produce a separate business entity. This means that you won't be able to separate your business assets and liabilities from your personal ones. This means that you will be personally liable for debts and obligations that stem from the business.

You will still be able to get a trade name, but it will be harder to raise money since you won't be able to sell stock, and banks are less likely to lend to sole proprietorships. However, this entity remains a good option for low-risk businesses and for those who want to test their business idea before forming a formal business.

PARTNERSHIP

This is a simple business structure for businesses owned by two or more people. There are two types of partnerships to choose from: limited partnerships and limited liability partnerships.

Limited partnerships (LPs) have a general partner with unlimited liability, and all other partners only have limited liability. Those with limited liability will also have limited control over the company, as outlined in a partnership agreement. Profits are reported on personal tax returns, and the partner without limited liability will need to pay self-employment taxes.

Limited liability partnerships (LLPs) are similar to LPs but give all owners limited liability. This means all partners are protected from debts against the partnership and aren't responsible for the actions of the other partners.

Partnerships are a good option for businesses with multiple owners, professional groups, and groups that want to assess the viability of a business idea before forming a formal business.

Limited Liability Company (LLC)

Forming an LLC gives you the benefits of both a corporation and a partnership business structure. You will be protected from personal liability, and your personal assets won't be at risk in case your business faces bankruptcy or lawsuits. Profits and losses can go through your personal income without being impacted by corporate taxes. However, the members of an LLC are treated as self-employed and must pay self-employment tax on both Social Security and Medicare.

In many states, LLCs can have a limited life. If a member joins or leaves an LLC, then some states may require the company to be dissolved and re-formed with a new membership. Unless there is a prior agreement to buy, sell, or transfer ownership.

Forming an LLC is a good idea for a medium- or higher-risk business, owners with a lot of personal assets to protect, and those who want to pay a lower tax rate than a corporation.

CORPORATION

A corporation is sometimes referred to as a C corp. This is a legal entity separate from the owners. A corporation can make a profit, be taxed, and be held legally liable. A corporation offers the greatest protection to owners from personal liability, but the cost of forming a corporation is often higher than that of other entities. There is also a greater requirement for record-keeping, operational processes, and reporting. Unlike the other entities, corporations pay income tax on profits. Sometimes corporate profits are taxed twice: once when the company earns a profit and again when dividends are paid to shareholders, who report them on their personal tax returns.

The corporation has an independent life aside from the shareholders. If a shareholder leaves the company or sells their shares, then the business can continue to operate undisturbed. Corporations also have an advantage in raising capital because they can raise funds through the sale of stock, which can help attract employees. Corporations are a good option for medium- or higher-risk businesses, those that need to raise money, and those who want to "go public" and eventually sell.

Another option is an S corporation (S corp). This is a special type of corporation that avoids the double taxation of a regular C corp. The S corporation's profits and some losses are passed through directly to the owners' personal income without being subject to corporate tax rates. However, not all S corporations are taxed equally by the states. Most S corporations are recognized by the federal government in the same way, and their shareholders are taxed accordingly. On the state level, some S corporations are taxed on profits above a specific limit, and others don't recognize the S corp at all and treat it as a C corp. An S corp needs to file with the IRS to obtain S corp status, which is separate from registering with the state.

An S corp also has special limits. They can't have more than 100 shareholders, and all of them need to be US citizens. You'll still need to follow the strict filing and operational requirements for a C corp. S corps also have an independent life like C corps. If a shareholder leaves the company or sells their shares, then the business can continue operating undisturbed. S corporations are a good choice for businesses that would normally be C corporations but meet the necessary criteria to be S corporations.

Lastly, there is also the option of a B Corp or a benefit corporation. These are for-profit corporations recognized by most US states. They differ from C corps in purpose, accountability, and transparency, but they are taxed the same as C corps. B Corps are focused on mission and profit. The shareholders hold the company accountable for producing a public benefit in addition to financial profit. Some states will require B Corps to submit annual benefit reports demonstrating their contributions to the public good.

Once you know the type of business entity you want to form and have completed the necessary forms, you are ready to register for taxes.

REGISTER FOR TAXES

Before you can open your business, you will need to register for a variety of state and federal taxes. To register for taxes, you'll need to apply for an EIN or

Employer Identification Number. This process is simple and free.

An EIN is also known as a Federal Employer Identification Number (FEIN) or Federal Tax Identification Number (FTIN). It is essentially the same as a Social Security Number (SSN) for your business. It is a unique nine-digit EIN that allows the Internal Revenue Service (IRS) to identify businesses for tax reporting purposes.

Request an EIN. You can go online to the IRS EIN Assistant website and simply follow the step-by-step application process once you have formed your business entity. There will be questions and answers to help you simplify the process.

You will need to form your business entity before you get an EIN. The IRS will need your business formation date and legal business name. You will also need to register your business and get approval for your business name from the state before you can get an EIN.

No matter what type of business you have, it is a good

idea to get an EIN number. Consider some of the benefits of getting an EIN number for your business:

> It will simplify the process of tracking and managing professional expenses.

> You will be able to build business credit.

> You can qualify for more business loans.

> You will need an EIN before you can hire employees.

> When forming an LLC, the EIN helps you maintain a corporate veil.

> An EIN prevents identity theft.

BANK ACCOUNT AND CREDIT CARD

When you own a business, it is critical that you have a dedicated business bank and credit account to protect your personal assets. If you mix your personal and business accounts, then your personal assets can be placed at risk if the business is ever sued. In business law terms, this means piercing the corporate veil.

OPEN A BANK ACCOUNT

When you open a business bank account, it separates your personal assets from the company's, protecting them. It will also help to make accounting and filing taxes easier.

GET A CREDIT CARD

This will help you keep personal and business expenses separate and keep all your business expenses in one place. It will also help build your business's credit history, making it easier to raise money and invest later.

PERMITS AND LICENSES

Most states will have some form of licensing requirement for a pet hotel. Typically, these are regulated under the state Department of Agriculture. There may be additional local laws, regulations, and inspections by counties and cities in order for a pet hotel to operate. Some common registrations you'll need include a sales tax permit, an EIN, and an occupancy permit.

What is a Business License?

In a broad sense, a business license is formal approval from a government agency that authorizes a business to operate legally within a specific jurisdiction. Some states will require a business to obtain a general state license, while others may require only a city license. It is more common for a business to need a city business license than a general state license.

The issue is that the term "business license" is often applied to other registrations as well, such as sales tax permits, resale certificates, and occupational permits. Typically, a business will need several licenses and permits to operate, depending on the type of business and the required level of licensing. Influencing factors include location, type of business, and what the business sells or does, which will determine licensing needs.

Let's look at some of the common business registrations

required by cities and states.

Occupancy Permits

To operate a business, zoning approval is often required for a commercial business location. In some areas, a business operating from a personal home will also need to obtain a home occupation permit.

Occupational or Professional Licensing

While this isn't specifically a business license, there are some occupations and professions that require you to get a license before offering a service. This can be both a local and state requirement, depending on your location. For a pet boarding business, you may need to adhere to local ordinances for licenses or permits.

Sales Tax Permits

This is required by states for businesses that sell products or offer certain services.

Resale Certificate

This is needed in order to avoid paying sales tax on inventory purchases.

Unemployment and Workers' Compensation Registration

This is often a requirement if a business plans to hire employees.

Insurance

As a responsible pet business owner, you likely have a lot of planning to do for the foreseeable crisis that can occur. However, there are still unimaginable and unplanned issues that can develop. As a pet hotel owner, you need to find a way to successfully and safely operate even in uncertain times. To do this, you need to consider an insurance plan to ensure you have adequate coverage for the worst-case scenario. Let's take a closer look at the level of insurance you need and what precautions you should take to avoid having to use your insurance.

What insurance is needed for a pet boarder? Unpredictable is commonplace in the pet business industry. You are caring for living animals that can't speak to you. While you can take every precaution, you can't prevent all challenges with certainty. This is where pet business insurance can help.

Rather than general business insurance, pet business insurance was created to help businesses in the pet industry. As with other insurance types, the goal is to invest in coverage without ever having to actually use it. Let's look at the policy itself to see how you can have adequate coverage for issues that may arise.

Challenges Facing the Pet Industry

At the time of writing, there is a public health crisis alongside an ongoing economic downturn. All of these affect both clients and pet care businesses.

Client and Pet Safety

While there are observable effects of COVID-19 in

humans, there are also conflicting accounts about how the virus can affect animals. This can make your clients more nervous about entrusting their animals to a stranger's care. This means you need to create a safe environment for both pets and their owners.

STAFF SAFETY

During COVID-19, it is recommended that people avoid in-person interaction. This can be a challenge in the pet industry. You need to implement social distancing protocols that will keep your staff safe.

LOSS OF BUSINESS

There is a decent chance that you'll experience a loss of business as a result of COVID-19. Whether from client apprehension, decreased staffing, or mandatory closure. This can make it challenging to cover expenses and successfully weather the crisis.

There are a few types of insurance to consider for your pet hotel business. There is general business coverage as well as pet business-specific coverage. Let's first consider pet care-specific coverage options.

Animal Floater/Bailee

This type of coverage will protect you if an animal dies in your care. This is to cover you for the absolute worst-case scenario.

Lost Key

If you provide any type of "house-calls" or provide walking services out of a client's home to avoid business premises, then this insurance is essential. This coverage will protect your business if an employee misplaces a client's key while providing household services.

Then there are basic business coverage options:

Commercial Liability

This will cover conflicts that can come from the general operations of a business. This is things such as a client slipping on spilled water and getting injured. Today, if a client contracts COVID-19 on your premises, then a lawsuit could follow. This insurance would cover the lawsuit and any resulting damage.

Worker's Compensation

This is important if you plan to hire employees. It is also important to ensure it covers you if an employee contracts COVID-19 while on the job.

Business Interruption

This coverage will help you during periods when you can't continue business operations. While some policies include virus-related continuity challenges, it is important to assess the level of coverage offered.

Operating Considerations

When it comes to starting a pet hotel, after you've finished all the paperwork, you'll need to consider a few areas of day-to-day operations before you officially get started. Let's consider these areas in greater detail.

Expenses

Some ongoing expenses to keep in mind include rent, standard facility costs, insurance, website maintenance, and marketing. Industry professionals suggest expecting at least $10,000 per month in expenses. The largest portion of the budget will be payroll costs. The overall monthly budget will vary based on facility size, the number of employees, and location.

REGULATIONS

Most states have regulations regarding kennels and pet hotels. These regulations are often linked to kennel construction, space, utilities, and maintenance. If you are going to start a pet hotel, you need to make sure your kennel space meets state code, especially if there are routine state inspections.

PERMITS AND ZONING

Before you build or move into a facility, you should make sure the building is zoned for that purpose. You should take the time to become familiar with your state's regulations for commercial kennel operations and then aim to go beyond these standards. This will ensure you not only meet the requirements but also help you get new clients.

SPACE

You should also make sure the building you choose has enough space to accommodate your potential clients. States may require a specific size housing area for each dog based on weight. For example, in the state of Connecticut, both inside and outside runs need to be at least 10 feet long and 36 inches wide for dogs up to 45 pounds, and at least 48 inches wide for dogs over 45 pounds.

CONSTRUCTION REQUIREMENTS

A pet hotel needs to be structurally sound, water-resistant, and non-toxic to avoid injury or escape of the pets in your care. You also need to prevent outside animals from entering and protect guests from inclement weather. There should be both hot and cold running water, a way to maintain a comfortable temperature for both dogs and your employees, and adequate ventilation and lighting at all times. Some states may even have specific lighting and/or temperature requirements, so you'll want to check in advance what requirements you need to meet. You should also have a separate facility to house dogs that need quarantine.

Sanitary Conditions

Ensure your employees can provide your guests with clean, fresh water and fresh food at all times. Plus, the dishes need to be kept clean and sanitary. There should be a way to clean up urine and feces, wash and disinfect the living areas, and dispose of waste in a sanitary manner. The area should be kept clean enough to avoid pests such as rats and mice.

Segregation

No more than one dog should be kept in a cage unless there is a health or welfare reason. For example, a mother dog needs to feed her puppies. A cage should allow a dog to stand up, turn around and lie down. Adult dogs should be segregated by sex to prevent breeding and protect them from injury or attacks.

Mitigating Liabilities

When it comes to liability issues in a pet hotel, there are some things you need to keep in mind in order to reduce these issues.

Keep All Areas Locked

The only people with access to your building should be employees who have keys or a PIN pad. This prevents clients and other outside people from entering areas that are unsafe for them or the pets in your care. Having areas blocked off will also allow you to control where pets go. However, you should still have several exit options in the event of an emergency.

Security Systems

You should have an overnight security system if you aren't going to have someone on the premises overnight. This can alert the police in the event of a break-in while also ensuring all pets remain in private accommodation, with motion sensors on your security system.

Staff Training

It is important that you ensure your staff follow all procedures so that pets are cared for safely and efficiently.

Cleaning Products

Make sure all cleaning products you use are safe for pets. When you maintain a clean environment, you will reduce the risk of infection and disease among the pets in your care. It is important to have a detailed cleaning procedure and schedule, as well as proper training for your staff.

Non-Refundable Deposit

Charging a deposit will eliminate last-minute cancellations and "no shows." This means you can save accommodations for those who really need them, and you won't be left with last-minute vacant spots. If there is a cancellation, you can consider offering store credit. This can increase profits while still allowing clients to get their money's worth if something comes up at the last minute, and a client can keep an appointment.

Company Policy

All company policies should be clearly displayed on your website and provided to clients during their check-in. These policies should list all important information for clients: prices, required shots, deposits, and more.

Signed Policy Sheet

Before you accept a pet into your facility, you should get a signed policy sheet. This sheet should explain all of the important policies and a waiver of liability to ensure you aren't held liable if something happens. Before you start a business, you should have this sheet reviewed and possibly even written by an attorney licensed to practice law in the same state as your business. This will reduce future legal issues and ensure clients can't claim they weren't informed of specific policies.

Confirm Pet Information

To make the job easier, double-check all notes before admitting a pet. This should include things like the owner's contact information, shot records, medication instructions, and any special diet instructions.

PRICING

When it comes to starting a pet hotel, one of the most important things to consider is how much you plan to charge clients per night for their animals to stay with you. While most pet hotels limit their boarding to dogs and cats, you can offer your services to a variety of animals as long as you have proper accommodations.

Often prices are set on a per-day basis and can range from $18-$28 per animal, depending on size and type. This will establish your base price and can include a specific amount of interaction with you or your staff. You can then offer additional services for an added fee. The first thing you need to do is make sure you price your services properly.

As in most markets, the costs of running a pet hotel have risen over the past year. In some areas, higher minimum wage requirements have significantly increased costs. As with most pet care business owners, you likely won't be comfortable raising prices later to stay ahead of increased costs. So, you need to make sure you adequately set your prices before you start. Understanding pricing and costs is critical to running a pet hotel and maintaining profitability.

There are many ways to determine your pricing. The first thing you need to do is determine your fixed and variable costs, then ensure you price your services above those costs so you still have some money left over to compensate you and anyone else invested in your business.

CALCULATE FIXED COSTS

These are the costs essential to operating your business, whether you have one or a hundred animals staying at your pet hotel. These would include mortgage or lease payments, infrastructure payments, property taxes, utilities, marketing, and management costs.

Estimate Variable Costs

These expenses can be adjusted as occupancy rates change. This includes things like labor, food, credit card fees, and others. You are attempting to determine how much more money each pet might be costing your business. Within the pet industry, most businesses can incorporate an extra pet or two without much added cost. However, additional staff may be required to care for a specific number of pets, and payroll costs can be high. Therefore, you need to project a realistic occupancy rate and use your best judgment to determine a reasonably accurate variable cost per day or night.

Combine Costs

To determine your total costs, multiply your estimated variable cost per night by your expected occupancy to get the total expected variable cost. Then you can add this to your estimated total fixed costs. This gives you a total estimated cost. Divide this by your expected occupancy in order to determine the estimated cost per night to charge.

Some people mistakenly use this number to develop a

price structure. However, keep in mind that you, as the owner, need to be paid, and you should also have some leftover money to cover unexpected expenses or make additional investments to help grow the business. Most people forget this step and therefore don't realize they are pricing their services lower than they should.

Pricing Model

What do you feel you should be charging people? What is a price the market can bear? Most privately owned businesses in the pet care industry determine their pricing by looking at competitors' prices and then pricing the same, less, or more.

If you are providing a higher level of care or additional amenities than your competitors, you should set your prices higher. However, if you are going to charge more, you will need to consistently explain or demonstrate to both prospective and existing clients why you are worth more. This should be done in a concise, compelling, and consistent manner. You can do this through visual imagery, including the building, marketing materials, staff appearance, and attention to detail. It should also be demonstrated in things people hear, such as the words and tone of your staff and the descriptions of your care and services.

The first chance you have to justify higher pricing is over the phone when prospects first call your hotel. Since pet care is a highly emotional business, prospective pet parents want to validate the pets they are considering caring for. How you handle the phone call will give them peace of mind that their pet is in good hands. It also gives you a chance to positively promote additional services that can improve the quality of a pet's stay.

Just make sure you don't fall for the myth that pricing your services less than the competition will send more clients to you. This is often untrue. In some cases, you may even lose potential customers who perceive a lower price as indicating lower quality.

Pricing Special Services

When you run a pet hotel, you will undoubtedly end up caring for a percentage of animals that require some level of extra care. Some examples include the following:

Immobile dogs

Puppies

Extra-large dogs that may require two people to lift

Dogs that require handling by training personnel only

Pets that require assistance expressing their bladders

Special diets

Diabetic pets

The logic and math are easy to see; the more labor and skills needed, as well as the greater the risk of injury to you and your staff, should equal a greater charge. When you charge more for these special care or services, you will be able to afford the quality staff and the extra time needed to provide proper care for these pets.

The issue is that the people who often start pet care businesses are the ones who are uncomfortable charging for these special care and services. Most feel it is their job to provide any level of care needed, at the same cost as for a healthy, low-maintenance pet. However, this isn't possible if you are going to have a sustainable and successful business.

It is important to remember that pet parents are willing to pay for their pet to have appropriate care, but often won't volunteer to pay more. Therefore, if you explain to the pet owner why you are charging additional fees and educate them, then they will be open to the extra costs.

Determining What to Charge

When it comes to medical services, you may want to check with local veterinarians to see what they would charge. You will probably charge a little less, since you may not have the same level of training or as many trained staff.

If you are offering additional services such as extra walks or mobility sessions, you could charge a base fee plus a markup percentage. If you only charged the actual cost, then you may overlook a few items and lose money on a pet's stay.

Providing an extra level of care will provide a client with peace of mind. Charging an appropriate amount relative to the level of care will provide your business with the revenue you and your staff deserve. Along these lines, it is important to consider what amenities you can offer.

AMENITIES TO OFFER

When determining the right amenities to offer, the best answer is to provide enough to make your business stand out from the competition. Let's consider some amenities you can add to your services.

24/7 STAFFING

Having staff on-site all the time not only provides added security but also provides pet owners with peace of mind. Customers will feel extra security knowing someone is watching their pet all night and ensuring they are comfortable and happy.

PLAY AREAS

This is another important amenity and area of your offering. You should have both indoor and outdoor playgrounds. There should be plenty of drainage to make cleaning easy, and all equipment should be made with durable finishes and be easy to clean.

BOARDING OTHER PETS

Lastly, you can consider boarding other pets rather than limiting yourself to dogs. In general, the pet hotel industry faces a shortage of cat and exotic pet boarding options. Every type of animal needs a place to stay when its owners are on vacation. So consider designing a few suites for animals to diversify the types of animals you board.

BUILDING YOUR FACILITY

CHOOSING A LOCATION

While a pet hotel doesn't necessarily need you to have a prime, high-traffic location, it is beneficial that you find a convenient location close to neighborhood clusters. However, many neighborhoods have noise ordinances, and opening a pet hotel in such areas can be a bit of a challenge.

Before you sign a lease or purchase a location for your pet hotel, you should make sure the zoning requirements allow you to legally operate in the area.

Building any kind of pet business structure is similar to planning out a road trip. You first need to identify where you are and where you are trying to go. Let's take a look at each step in the process, starting with choosing your ideal location.

To get started, you want to write down everything that you want to have in your new pet hotel. You don't have to put anything in any particular order; just build the list as things come to mind. Don't leave anything off, and be as specific as possible. Consider both the inside and outside of the building.

Once you feel you have a complete list, you can rewrite it, grouping all the items together so you can expand on each use. Work through each area of the building and add anything that you may have missed on the original list. Once the list is organized by room and complete, then you'll have a decent idea of the size of the building you'll need for your pet hotel. From here, you can focus on finding a location for your new business. Now comes the question of renting, buying, or building your new pet hotel.

For a new pet hotel, location is key. Most businesses rely on visibility, and locating yourself on a major road is a great way to increase visibility. However, these types of properties often come at a premium price and are subject to zoning restrictions. If this is the case, then they may not be the best place to put your new pet hotel. There are other factors you need to consider before purchasing any piece of land or an existing building to set up your pet hotel.

Looking at your previous list, consider all the uses for your pet hotel and how they will fit into a property. Does your zoning district allow for both indoor and outdoor kennel runs? If not, you may need to ensure all activities are indoors, which will change your building requirements to meet all the needs on your list. If both indoor and outdoor kennels are permitted, is there sufficient space to provide a safe, secure area for the potential client base you hope to house? Is there room for growth if you need to add additional space in a few years?

BUYING VS. LEASING

Once you have an ideal location in mind, you need to consider whether to buy or lease it. Buying a building will be less complicated than leasing. You simply need to agree on a price with the seller and sign a contract. You have full control over the appearance of the building, but you'll also have the hassles of owning a property. Perhaps the biggest downside to purchasing a building is that commercial real estate typically takes longer to sell, and if your business fails, this can add stress. Also, purchasing a building will provide you with better cash flow than leasing. With lower interest rates and generous loan terms, purchasing can sometimes be less costly than leasing.

On the other hand, leasing a commercial property provides you with flexibility that you don't have when purchasing. If your business doesn't work out or you end up needing to change your square footage, you don't have to worry about selling a building. While cash flow is often tight in the early years of a new business, a leased property will cover you should there be any major repairs needed.

If you are going to sign a commercial lease agreement, then you should have an attorney review it. Landlords will have a lot of experience compared to you, and you don't want them to take advantage of you. Spending a few hours of an attorney's time can be a small investment towards the future success of your business. Commercial leases will require a security deposit, along with first- and last-month lease payments.

When it comes to choosing a location, as with most decisions surrounding the start of a business, it requires thorough research. You can use the local small-business community, chamber of commerce, city economic developer, and others to ensure you are making the right location choice.

LOOKING FOR A PROPERTY

Whether you choose to buy or lease, there are many factors to consider when deciding on a location. It is a good idea to consult with a commercial real estate agent early in the process. As things develop, you may also need to consult with a real estate attorney. All businesses have special needs, but none more so than a pet hotel. A commercial real estate agent will have the training and knowledge needed to find a property specific to your needs.

Zoning regulations will prevent you from simply building a pet hotel anywhere. For example, a pet hotel likely won't be permitted within a residential zoning district. There may even be requirements that a pet hotel be located in a rural, commercial, industrial, or even agricultural district. The specific zoning requirements vary by municipality. A commercial real estate agent will help you sort through these requirements and find you the right location that provides you with enough room for any future growth.

Once you have the building and location dialed in, you can focus on the equipment you need on hand before you start operating your business.

Equipment

If you are going to build a pet hotel from the ground up,

then you will need a lot of equipment to help you run smoothly day to day. Consider some of the equipment you'll need just to offer clients the basic amenities:

- Cages, crates, and small protected areas

- Indoor exercise and/or play area

- Dog toys

- Grooming table

- Drinking and eating bowls

- Treats

- Office space and associated equipment such as laptop, chairs, table and more

- Pool and/or training course

- Beds and rest areas

Waste disposal system and/or area

In addition, your entire property needs to be secured. You should have security cameras in place around the facility. For health and safety, you'll also need to ensure the property is well ventilated.

Once you have everything planned and ready, you can start the construction process, which comes with its own set of decisions to make.

THE CONSTRUCTION PROCESS

CHOOSING A BUILDING

Before you purchase an existing building and start your renovations, there are some things you need to consider. When you purchase an existing building, you probably won't have much if any construction documents available. If there are drawings, then they may not reflect alterations, additions, or renovations made to the structure. Some documents that can be helpful to you would be the floor plan, wall sections, and information on the infrastructure such as the mechanical system, electrical, plumbing, and structural components.

In order to set priorities, you'll need to have a budget and to know the level of renovations you need to make. Some areas to consider investigating with evaluating the building before purchasing and renovating include the following:

    Zoning and land use for the site

    Environmental studies

    Mechanical system, including all ductwork

    Roof system

    Thermal insulation

    Acoustical components

    Americans with Disabilities Act (ADA) compliance

Drainage and slab work

Life safety

We've already discussed the importance of zoning issues, so let's look at the others in a little greater detail.

Environmental Studies

Environmental studies will determine whether there is any asbestos or lead-based paint, as well as any site contamination. The permitting entity is going to require this information, and you'll need a mitigation plan for any asbestos or lead-based paint before you are able to start renovations. If there are site contamination issues, such as soil or groundwater contamination, you'll need to fully understand the extent of the contamination and your legal responsibilities for assuming liabilities before you choose to purchase.

Mechanical Systems

The condition and capacity of the mechanical building

system are important to know because correcting any issues can be costly. Many buildings were once used for simple functions like retail, office, or warehousing. This means the heating, ventilation, and air conditioning (HVAC) system won't be sized to meet the ventilation and humidity requirements typical of a pet hotel business. In addition, undersized and old HVAC systems will also not meet new energy codes.

Other issues may include the units being in the wrong location and having undersized ductwork. The ductwork itself may be made of outdated duct board with insulation on the inside lining. This type of ducting will collect pet hair and odors, making them nearly impossible to remove. This type of ductwork will need to be completely replaced before you can begin operations.

Roofing System

The existing roof system is one of the first aspects you should review. This applies to all types of roofs that can present their own problems: flat, metal, and shingle roofs. Know how old the roof is, or ask if it was replaced recently. If there is a new roof, find out if it is still under warranty. Know how to transfer the warranty to your business. Look for any signs of roof leaks. Also, ensure there is enough roof insulation to meet current energy codes.

Thermal Insulation

A quick analysis of the building envelope can be done by a mechanical engineer, architect, or contractor to determine the thermal properties of the walls and roof system. A roofing contractor can also take a core sample of the roof insulation to confirm the thickness. The wall properties are confirmed by thermal infra-red imaging, but they can also be determined through a small amount of demolition. With energy code requirements, you may need to add more insulation in both the roof/ceiling space and the wall/window construction as part of your renovation process.

Acoustical Components

In any animal care business, noise control is a very important factor. Depending on previous use, there are likely no existing walls, doors, windows, or frameworks that have acoustical control properties. If you are going to keep any interior walls, you'll probably need to add additional construction to supplement the existing work. The simplest option is to replace interior walls and door systems with ones that have acoustical properties. Double-paned windows are more energy-efficient and help control noise. If there is a suspended ceiling system, then you should check above it. Walls that extend to the roof deck can help to contain any noise. Ceiling tiles can be easily replaced with new ones that have a higher NRS (noise reduction coefficient) rating.

AMERICANS WITH DISABILITIES ACT (ADA) COMPLIANCE

The permitting entity will likely require that a certain percentage of renovation construction costs be allocated to updating the facility to meet ADA requirements. There may be simple design requirements to accommodate this, but you shouldn't be surprised to hear about these requirements.

The entire facility should meet ADA requirements for both clients and staff. Different levels within the facility need to be evaluated. Complying with ADA requirements can be a little tricky if you have a two-story building. You will often need to include an elevator if there isn't one already in place, which can easily add $50,000 to the cost of the renovations.

Drainage and Slab Work

As you tour the building, look for the existing floor drains and consider where you may need to add new ones. Any new drains will require existing slab work to be cut and piping connected to the nearest sewer line. The connections are often located outside the building. The more drains you need to install, the more slab cutting will be required. You can talk with an architect about how you can reduce the amount of concrete you need to remove.

Cutting the concrete slab work to add more drains can be a complicated renovation. It can be even more complicated in a pre-engineered metal building. The main structural columns often have a reinforcement called "hairpins." This reinforcement is located in the concrete foundations and keeps the steel structure from splaying outward. These should never be cut or removed.

LIFE SAFETY

Lastly, if you plan to be in the building during renovations, then you need to keep the fire code in mind. The fire code requires that you always have a direct means of egress. Everyone needs to be safe while in the building. Your architect or contractor can help you keep operations running smoothly while planning a logical construction sequence and avoiding any permit issues that may arise from life-safety requirements.

Once you've considered all these requirements, you are ready to move on to the next stage, which is considering the construction process itself.

THINGS TO CONSIDER BEFORE CONSTRUCTION

The biggest question when constructing your pet hotel is whether you should work with the architect or the contractor first. With so many rules and regulations governing commercial property, it is important to use the services of a licensed architect, engineer, and commercial contractor. How you assemble a design and construction team will largely depend on how you want to "deliver" the project. The project delivery method will be determined by the legal contracting arrangements among the owner, the design entity, and the construction entity. Each entity will have its own role, and understanding the differences in delivery methods will help you to find and quality the right construction and design team for your new pet hotel.

Owner, architect/engineer, and contractor each play a role. There will be more team members within each of these areas, but each will fall under one of these three main areas. Consider some brief descriptions of the main team member roles and responsibilities:

> The owner determines the initial budget parameters and maintains the financial resources to finish the project

> The owner is also responsible for communicating their goals for the project and maintaining the contracts for services

> The design team creates documents used for

permitting and construction

The contractor builds and provides project warranties

The architect ensures that the construction meets the design intent and meets code requirements

The design team will provide observation of the construction, rather than supervision: there is a legal difference between the two, and the general contractor is responsible for supervision

The contractor is legally responsible for everything related to construction

The contractor is also responsible for safety on the site

COMMON PROJECT DELIVERY METHODS

The three most common project delivery methods to consider are the following:

Design-Bid-Build (D-B-B)

Design-Build (D-B)

Construction Manager or CM at Risk

There are other options, but these are the three most often used for pet hotel-sized projects. Let's consider each in greater detail.

Design-Bid-Build (D-B-B) - Also known as the "low bid" method of choosing a contractor, this is the most recognizable method and most commonly used by governments. It is also a strict method since it is a formalized process. It is mandatory that all bidders price the same information and provide bids at a designated time and place.

This method requires that the construction documents be complete before the bidding process. These documents are used by each general contractor to form the basis for the bid. Subcontractors, such as plumbers and suppliers, will provide bids to multiple general contractors bidding on the overall project. Consider the following components of this method.

The owner gets bids from multiple contractors based on a set of bid documents from the architect and engineers.

The construction contract is concluded between the owner and the contractor. The contract is often based on the lowest bid, but it isn't a requirement. A contractor may also be chosen based on the "most responsive" bid, as determined by the provided documents.

This method relies on cost estimates during design until actual bids are obtained through a highly competitive bidding process.

Low bids may incentivize changes to orders as a means to increase construction costs once the bid is awarded.

The design team will have a separate contract for the design and construction phase services. Each of these contracts is made with the owner.

Keeping these procedures separate may lead to finger-pointing if conflicts arise between the architect and contractor. This may leave you feeling in the middle as the owner.

There is a system of checks and balances in place if the owner also contracts for bidding and construction observation services from the design team. To save money, some owners may choose to forgo these services. This level of risk should only be assumed by owners who are very familiar with the design and construction business. If you are getting a bank loan, then the lender may require you to include these construction observation services. Some states also have regulatory requirements that mandate architects to provide construction observation to monitor code compliance.

Design-Build - This is the method in which the owner selects a team comprising a contractor, architect, and engineer as a single entity. Interviews are often conducted with various prospective team members. As with the previous method, the choice is often made based on price. You will need to clearly communicate your construction budget and discuss whether the team is able to deliver what you want within that price. Consider the following components of this method.

The team that includes both the contractor and the design team will be under a single contract. Since the team is one entity, conflicts can be resolved more easily.

Most teams are led by the contractor, and they may drive the design process. During the design phases, cost estimating and value engineering efforts will start early.

Once the design phase is finished, a Guaranteed Maximum Price (GMP) will be established. This is what you would expect to pay for the actual construction of the building.

You'll still get the cost-saving benefits of bidding, since the general contractor will receive bids from subcontractors.

Since the contractor and design team are tied together, there will be less oversight. This means substitutions of materials and equipment can be made without the owner's knowledge.

This method also minimizes the risk of orders being missed by the architect or the contractor, as the documents will be developed jointly by the contractor and the design team.

Owners often appreciate that they only need to deal with one entity. However, this also means the owner will need to be more vigilant in overseeing the project, especially during construction.

Construction Manager (CM) At-Risk - With this method, the contractor is selected early in the project design phase and is a key team member, an equal partner with the owner and the architect/engineer. The success of this method relies on a balance of power and responsibility among the three entities.

Choosing this method may cost a little more since you are getting valuable pre-construction services from the contractor. The benefits you'll receive include more accurate cost estimates and value engineering early in the design process. If you have to make changes, you won't incur re-design fees from the architect or engineers. Consider the following components of this method.

The owner has separate contracts with the design team

and construction manager.

The CM is involved in value engineering and the design process.

The CM is involved in developing the design documents, making it easier to spot inconsistencies, omissions, or discrepancies early in the process.

You can still get cost-saving benefits from bidding, since the contractor can receive bids from subcontractors before final costs are determined.

Before construction starts, you can determine a GMP.

There will be fewer order changes.

SELECTING AND QUALIFYING THE CONTRACTOR AND DESIGN TEAM

If you want to find the most qualified architect and contractor for your pet hotel, you need to use a selection process that minimizes subjectivity and maximizes objectivity. You should try to make an apples-to-apples comparison and consider what value-added services each entity offers. Evaluate, rank, and choose based on qualifications and then negotiate the fee later. If you rank your choices and are unsuccessful in negotiating a price with your first choice, then you can move to the second one on your list.

If you are already working with an architect or engineer, then they may be able to help you find and qualify a contractor. You should choose a contractor that has project experience similar in size and complexity to yours. Most contractors have an established relationship with architects and can help you with assembling a design team if needed.

Another option is to use a formal Request for Qualifications (RFQ) selection process. This is a method that allows you to collect and compare similar information about several design teams or contractors.

You can also get referrals from others in the industry, friends, your lender, or professional associations. You can then interview the options to find a good fit. You should look for previous, related project experience along with qualities like compatibility and likability.

The key to choosing a design and construction team is having a basic understanding of the project delivery methods and choosing one that best fits your personality and individual needs. If you have a preference for one method over the other, then that will help you choose a contractor and/or architect first.

Once you've made the decision, you can start preparing for the construction process.

Preparing for the Construction Process

When it comes to building your pet hotel, the total cost of your renovations and/or construction should make economic sense. It is easy to come up with a long wish list, but you need to be mindful of your budget and return on investment. Let's look at some important areas to consider and where you need to be careful in your selection.

FUNCTIONALITY

Labor costs in the pet industry can average between 30 and 50 percent of the gross revenue. Operations and procedures, and how the staff implement them, will be critical to the design and bottom line. Most operators don't run their place in the same way, so you'll want to be both individual and successful. However, it also means you need to find a designer who understands your vision.

DURABILITY

Keeping your budget in mind is important. However, you should never cut expenses on construction materials that will hold up. Different finishes will be required throughout various areas of your facility. For example, you'll want a nice porcelain floor in the lobby, while choosing something durable and easy to clean for the main kennel area. Dogs cause extreme wear and tear on flooring, so it is important to choose materials that will hold up in enclosures and high-use areas.

When it comes to making choices, you should do as much research as possible on facilities that offer the same services as you. Consider their building and the construction to see how well it has held up over time. If possible, even find out their cleaning protocol. All this information can help you when filling in the operations section of your business plan.

The important thing is to avoid becoming overwhelmed with the process. Resist the temptation to go from idea to construction. While the project is still in the paper planning phase, you need to research and make choices carefully to avoid costly mistakes later. Each step needs to be taken in sequence, and you shouldn't be afraid to go back and revise things until the project reaches its final form. You will be truly happy with the efforts. Consider one of the major areas, the layout of your building. It may be simple, but there is a lot that goes into it.

BUILDING LAYOUT

One of the daily challenges a pet hotel can face is the facility layout. The layout of a building is key to a business's efficiency and productivity. If you are purchasing an existing building, you may not have much say in this area at first. On the other hand, if the layout is so ineffective, you may want to consider gutting the building and rebuilding it as part of the renovation process. If you are able to build a new facility, then you can have an easier time doing this.

When you look to build a new pet hotel, there is no shortage of architects, engineers, and consultants who know the proper layout and its impact on efficiency and productivity. It can be helpful to consult with a successful facility operator with years of experience and/or firsthand knowledge of the pet industry.

If you have an existing facility, you may feel it isn't much you can do to improve efficiencies. This can't be further from the truth. Take the time to analyze the daily workflow and procedures to see where and how you can make adjustments. Consider a flowchart of common functions performed throughout the day. Timing and charting movements are key to identifying areas for improvement.

Once you have all the data you need, review the common routes taken and the time needed to perform common functions. This will also help you to see where procedures need to be changed.

Having an efficient, well-defined workflow is key to reducing unnecessary labor costs. In addition, it will help reduce disturbance and stress on the pets in your care. When choosing a layout for your building, consider the following common tasks and strategies to improve your facility's efficiency and productivity.

CLEANING

This is perhaps the largest part of the daily labor expense at a pet hotel. You should ensure your staff have the right equipment and materials. Plus, there should be adequate cleaning stations and storage areas in convenient locations throughout your facility.

FEEDING

Food prep stations that are centrally located or convenient have helped reduce travel distance. Another option is to deliver pet food by cart rather than make individual trips. At a pet hotel, animals are often fed twice a day. If you don't have an organized plan, you may find your staff making needless, wasteful trips back and forth to the food area.

Outdoor Access

Access to an outdoor area for eliminations is important. It is just as important to have access to these areas from the boarding rooms, with direct, short routes. This is also important should the need arise to evacuate the building.

Check-In and Out

Better customer service and more efficient operations can be achieved by strategically locating holding areas at the front of your facility for animals arriving and departing. This reduces the need to head to the back of the building, which disturbs the boarding pets and the animal going home. If you can acquire departure times at check-in, then you can bring these animals to the front prior to departure.

You can also hold arriving animals for a brief period until

staff is available and/or the time is appropriate to take them to their regular enclosure. Keep in mind that time is money, and anything you can do to make your operation more productive and efficient will positively impact your bottom line.

FLOORING

This is likely one of the most difficult decisions you will face when constructing your pet hotel. Whether you are building a new facility, renovating an existing building, or remodeling a current building, choosing the right flooring for indoor areas can be a very overwhelming task. With so many options available, it can be difficult to make the right decision.

The first thing you need to do is consider the key attributes of your flooring and the role it will play in indoor areas.

Clean-Ability: One of the most required attributes of flooring is that it is easy to clean and slip-resistant. Since indoor rooms are one of the busiest and most used areas of your pet hotel, you need to have a safe area for both staff and boarding animals. Most standard flooring options will overcompensate for slipping with a textured surface. However, this will make it more difficult to clean and maintain.

Durable Yet Soft: The floor surface should be easy to stand and walk on all day while also reducing fatigue. A more pliable floor will give dogs traction and added safety, since it gives a little underfoot. The unfortunate trade-off with nearly all flooring options is that softness doesn't align with long-term durability.

Seamless: Having a seamless option is key in animal care facilities, especially for daycare rooms. Since these rooms are often heavily used, the likelihood of accidents increases. Any floor surface with open seams can be problematic. Welded seams are an option, but seam integrity can be compromised if they aren't installed properly, and the stability of the underlying surface is affected. Seams are also an area where mold, mildew, and bacteria can grow. If fluids penetrate, this area can also become home to smells that never go away.

Aesthetics: Choosing a flooring option that is visually

appealing can boost employee morale and also appeal to pet owners. Often, the nicer the flooring, the more motivated employees will be to maintain a clean and professional environment.

Noise: Kennel spaces can be noisy. Hard floor surfaces can allow sound waves to continue around the room and don't lower the decibels. Soft floors will absorb noise and reduce decibel levels. Quieter rooms benefit both employees and clients, as dogs remain calm and less agitated in quieter environments.

Once you have considered the main attributes of your flooring, the next step is to evaluate your options and determine which best meets your needs.

Rubber Matting: This is a non-slip surface when you first install it. It is a comfortable option and is relatively easy to clean and maintain. It also has sound-deadening properties to minimize noise. The material is permanently glued to the floor with different options. A topical sealant can then be applied to provide a water-resistant surface and keep the floors clean and free of bacterial buildup. The downside is that not all sealants are the same, and most will degrade over time and require reapplication. If you don't keep on top of this reapplication, then you will eventually need to replace the flooring mats.

One of the main complaints about this option is that dogs can dig into it, causing divots. Also, there is a chance that a dog's feet can become black from the matting. Seams are also the weak link, and once a seam separates, then the floor deteriorates more quickly. Building up the sealant on the floor can also create a slick surface and make the floor harder. A dog's nails can also scratch the sealant.

Sometimes, the local Department of Agriculture or other regulating authorities may have restrictions on the types of floors that can be used in general kennel areas. You may need to remove rubber matting and replace it with non-porous surface options. While rubber matting is a high-traction option, the flooring can cause injuries when dogs stop too quickly, leading to tears in ligaments and/or joints. Other common issues include odor absorption and fading that can occur when rubber matting is exposed to ultraviolet light.

Artificial Grass: While often installed outdoors, artificial grass can also be a good option for indoor use. If you're using artificial grass as a long-term solution, you need to follow all the manufacturer's recommendations. When used indoors, artificial grass often suffers from odor problems, cleaning difficulties, and other installation-related issues. This is not an issue with the grass but rather with installation or with choosing the wrong type. If installed properly, it will provide a great, safe option for dogs and, in some models, a hygienic option with built-in antimicrobial agents. When you install artificial grass indoors, you'll need a good drainage system underneath and the grass elevated on a platform.

Seamless Anti-Fatigue Flooring Systems: These are fast becoming the newest trend in flooring at animal facilities. These floors are available in a range of thicknesses and can be made in a combination of epoxy, rubber matting, rubber pellets, or vinyl flake, along with a flexible, seamless topcoat. These floors offer the benefit of reducing stress on the joints and muscles of dogs and their human caretakers. In addition, these floors will reduce sound decibels while being decorative, functional, and cost-effective. You can also adjust the texture on demand to provide an anti-skid surface that prevents paw pad injuries while remaining easy to clean. These floors are non-porous and require little maintenance; you don't have to wax or continually seal them.

As with other types of flooring, good installation is key to success. HVAC plays a critical role in removing moisture and humidity from the area. Since the floors are non-porous, moisture from the air won't soak into them. If the humidity is too high, condensation will sit on the surface and make it feel wet. Before installation, it is key to test and measure the moisture content and vapor transmission in concrete.

The type of flooring you choose for your building will ultimately be determined by your intended use, ease of cleaning, desired aesthetics, and overall budget. As you can see, there are many options available, and determining what is best for your business will depend on your wants, needs, and desires. Just remember to budget for professional installation, as it's important for nearly all flooring types.

One area where new pet hotel owners often overlook is the different needs of animals. Often, a pet hotel or boarding facility has a basic layout and furnishes it based on animal needs. However, if you want to offer the best options to your clients and increase your chances of getting additional borders, then you need to prepare for each animal species you plan to house. Many forget to focus on cats and to set up the proper facilities for them. So let's look at how you can prepare your facility to house cats.

Focus on Cats

Why Board Cats

Before you can prepare your facility to board cats, you should first consider the importance of why your facility should board cats. There are plenty of reasons people want to board their cats, but many owners have a hard time leaving them in a place they feel doesn't offer the most desirable environment for a cat.

Using existing space in your building and without a large budget, you can easily add a significant profit center to your pet hotel. Customers who want to board cats are looking for a pleasant-looking, pleasant-smelling place that is comfortable for their cats. Does this describe the current view of your cat boarding facility, or do you think there is room for you to improve? Perhaps you don't offer this service because you haven't discovered its benefits. So, let's first look at the why of boarding cats and improving your facility to accommodate them, and then we'll look at the how of adding the necessary components to board cats and bring in additional clients.

CLIENTS WHO BOARD CATS

Everyone in the industry knows that people are less likely to board cats than dogs. This is often because cats are viewed as self-sufficient and tend to be more finicky when placed anywhere other than their home. However, this doesn't mean you shouldn't invest in a boarding space that is appealing to cats and their owners. Simply putting some strategy into the design phase can help encourage people to board their cats at your pet hotel. Even if you only have a small room to set aside for boarding cats, you can turn this into a major business profit center.

People will be open to boarding cats for a range of reasons. Some people board cats for medical reasons, such as daily shots or other medical care. The most common are cats that need subcutaneous fluids for kidney issues or insulin shots for diabetes. Other people may choose to board cats if they are moving or showing their home to buyers and don't want to risk indoor-only cats getting outside. Still, others will need long-term lodging options for their cats because they don't like leaving their cats home alone for extended periods, whether due to elimination issues or simply to monitor their cat's well-being and interaction. As you can see, there are a number of reasons why people need or want to board a cat. However, many people have trouble leaving their cats at a basic boarding facility.

When designing a space for cats, the bottom line is to show owners that your priority and focus are on the cats. Have a nice, clean space and a program in place specifically for cats. Accommodations need to show owners that their cats are staying at a home away from home. So, let's consider some design options to help you create a space that appeals to both your clients and their cats.

DESIGNS FOR CATS

When most people hear terms like a kennel, boarding, or pet hotel, they assume you are referring to a place for dogs. However, by definition, most city zoning ordinance defines a kennel as any building that houses three or more animals. So, this means that any animals can be housed in a kennel or boarding facility. When it comes to cats, the more accurate term may be "cattery". When planning a facility to house cats, there are specific design considerations unique to cats that you need to focus on.

Cats are typically housed in condominium enclosures. Often, these "condos" are stacked two or three units high and have a separate combined living/sleeping/hiding area, along with a second compartment for the litter box and access for cleaning. Let's consider this condo design as the first step in preparing your hotel to accept cats.

Having a metal grill on the front of the condo allows the air to circulate. Some brands allow you to incorporate air channels to deliver continuous filtered air throughout the condo via the building's mechanical system. While this latter option may be more costly, it will also be more effective at preventing the spread of airborne disease. As the air leaves the cat condo, it will be drawn into the return air duct and then exhausted to the outside.

When it comes to the enclosure itself, there are many finish options. You shouldn't use unfinished or finished wood, as it can't be properly cleaned. The most common condo finish is melamine-covered wood, but it won't last as a long-term finish. Melamine is also known to sag under its own weight. This means that with a heavier cat, your condo's lifespan will be further shortened.

Fiberglass condos will provide you with a more durable finish. The surface is also a little more comfortable for cats as well. While easy to clean, fiberglass will scratch over time. Another option is stainless steel. This is a great option for isolation rooms since it is easy to clean, scratch-resistant, and will likely last for years. However, stainless steel will be the more costly option.

No matter what finish you choose, it should be water-resistant and easy to clean. Any metal grill should be made from aluminum or stainless steel. Painted, powder coating, or other finishes likely won't stand up to years of abuse in a pet hotel setting.

Clear-tempered glass or plastic rear panels can allow light to enter the condo if backed up to a window. Condos should also offer a shelf perch or two for lounging. With proper positioning, this can give cats a view of birds in the yard. It is also important to position the cattery in a location that considers barking noise from the kennel. The cattery should never be a passageway connecting other spaces in your building. If possible, the cattery and kennel should be separated by other quiet spaces. This and other things should be considered when planning the area around the cat condo.

Outside the Condo Considerations

During daytime hours, cats may be let loose in the cattery. In these situations, having wall-mounted shelves or tubes that wrap around the room can allow each cat to find an ideal place while away from home. While many of these products are commercially available, you can also consider making your own. There are plenty of design options online.

The main concern you need to consider is the safety of the animals and the caretakers. Make sure the walking surface has sufficient traction for any planned activities. Make sure items are mounted securely on the wall and wide enough for even the largest cats to lounge comfortably.

Drainage Issues

When planning a cattery, you also need to consider installing floor drains. Drains are an important part of a pet hotel, but wet cat litter can swell and clog them. Mops are not ideal in a pet hotel setting because they can spread dirt and germs. Floor drains in a cattery without a hair trap will cause plumbing problems at some point. You should make sure a hair trap is inspected weekly or more often as needed.

Ceiling Considerations

One of the overlooked design areas of a cattery is the

ceiling. Most commercial spaces use grid ceilings. These are cheap and allow you quick access to the equipment above the ceiling. Water-resistant ceiling tiles are even more inviting. However, a curious cat perched high on a catwalk may find some way into the attic space. Once you have a cat in the void above the ceiling grid, it can be nearly impossible to retrieve them, especially if they have no intention of getting caught. This is why a cattery should ideally have a hard ceiling with high-mounted catwalks.

Air Quality

In most office buildings, the air is continually re-circulated. In the winter, this air is warmed and sent throughout the building. Cats are prone to Upper Respiratory Infections (URIs), more so than dogs. As we mentioned early, the air in cattery units needs to be exhausted outside. The air from a cattery shouldn't be reused anywhere else in the building. A proper HVAC system will prevent air from the cattery or any isolation unit from being reused in the building.

Consider a Screened Porch

In fair weather, giving cats access to fresh air is important. A heavy mesh cat enclosure will protect cats from getting loose and prevent predators from entering. The conventional screen material isn't safe enough.

Important Components

We've looked at the important design components for a cattery. But you also need to consider what makes the space appealing for both clients and their cats. This includes things like clean spaces, odor elimination, comfort, activities, and distractions. Let's look at each of these things in greater detail.

Clean Spaces

Cleanliness is highly important for cats. Anyone who has been around cats knows how much they like to clean themselves and their surroundings. A clean facility also speaks volumes to your prospective clients and shows them that you are committed to the wellness and comfort of the pets under your care.

You can make cleaning easier by also using cat boarding condos made from materials that are easy to clean and don't absorb urine. You also want to choose materials that are durable enough to withstand pressure washing for easy cleanup of larger messes. It is a good idea to pressure wash the cat condos at least a few times a year.

You should also make sure that cat condos are easy to move. This can make it easier to take them outside for pressure washing or to move them around within the facility to clean behind and under them regularly.

Odor Elimination

If you choose materials that don't absorb odors for your cat condos, you are already partway toward eliminating odors in your facility. Another factor that helps eliminate odor is proper ventilation. The smaller the area, the more important proper ventilation is. The fewer odors cats can smell from other cats, the happier they'll be.

The best practice for odor elimination is to remove the

odor source as soon as possible. This means you should have a staff member checking on the cat condos often and removing messes as soon as they occur.

It is also important to have an exhaust system running in the cat area of your pet hotel. It can be a little more expensive, but having an exhaust system built right into the cat condos can ensure air is exhausted right at the source. Even an exhaust fan running continuously in the cat room will help remove odors and keep the space smelling cleaner.

Comfort

A clean, odorless environment will go a long way toward cat comfort, but there are other things that can help prioritize comfort for cats. The best philosophy when housing cats is to mimic the "home away from home" as much as you can. The separation of living space can greatly increase the cats' comfort level.

Other comfortable factors include the materials and design of the condos. The material you choose needs to be gentle on the cats' paws, and the walls need to offer privacy so the cats can't see their neighbors. Add in a cat's favorite bed, food, or litter, and they'll feel just like they are at home.

ACTIVITIES AND DISTRACTIONS

It can be a good idea to have a water fountain or other background noise in the cat room, perhaps some relaxing music. Windows that let cats watch birds or other wildlife in the backyard can also provide relaxing sights and sounds. You can include a cat program that has playtime, cuddle time, and catnip toys or treats. For some cats, outdoor time in strollers or screened-in areas is a great way to get fresh air each day. These are all additional items that people can add to their cat's stay.

Now you can see that there isn't a lot that goes into designing a specific cat boarding space. However, the additional profits from these small changes can have a big impact on your pet hotel business. So, when you are designing and building your new venture, make sure you take time to focus on the cats as well.

Another aspect of running a pet hotel to consider is the

software you need. Everything runs on computers and electronics today. Having the right software can streamline operations and make it easier to run a pet hotel business.

HELPFUL SOFTWARE

Analog methods for managing a pet hotel quickly become ineffective as you grow. So, it is best to invest in the right software from the moment you start your pet hotel and let it grow with your business. However, if you are new to the pet industry or want to improve your current facility, you may not be familiar with this type of software. When looking for a software solution, you should start by evaluating your customers and staff. Let's consider some of the features you need to look for in a software solution for your pet hotel.

Client and Pet Management

Software should include unlimited client profiles with photos. There should be a support system for paperless waivers and other signed documents. Hidden internal staff notes are important for specific clients. You also want quick, easy access to medical and vaccination records.

Customer Portal and Online Booking

Software should be mobile-friendly to enable digital signing of waivers and uploading of records. You can streamline processes if the software can collect deposits online. Owners will enjoy a customer portal to view photos and videos of their pets. Online booking that allows owners to customize the services, features, and forms will also make the process easier and impress potential clients.

Reservation Management Features

Software should make it easy for clients to customize reservation types. Viewing of appointment availability should be easier for both staff and clients. Software should also simplify the check-in/check-out process and ensure you have all the information you need to provide pets with a safe stay while in your care.

Key Communication Features

Clients appreciate automated communications for confirming appointments and receiving reminders. This can also allow you to provide small customer service details, such as vaccination reminders and report cards. Plus, it will save your staff time by eliminating the need to manually send out communications.

Retail Features

Software should also be usable as a point-of-sale system. This allows you to offer add-on services and retail products to improve your business's profitability.

Marketing Features

The best software can also send SMS and email marketing communications. Making this process quicker and easier for your business. It should also allow you to easily filter your customers and customize the necessary communications.

Staff Management Features

Some important features of the software in the staff management area include personalized to-do lists, commission tracking, a time clock with associated reports, and even the ability to schedule specialists such as groomers and trainers. These things will help improve and make internal processes and operations easier.

Choosing the right software as you start your pet hotel can help set up your business for success. The right software allows you to cut down on staff costs, reduce the risk of errors, and help you stand out from the competition in customer service. As you get closer to opening your pet hotel, the next major area to consider is how you will market your business to attract new clients and retain existing ones.

SUGGESTED SOFTWARE

https://www.gingrapp.com/

http://kennellink.com/

https://www.pawfinity.com/

https://www.revelationpets.com/

MARKETING YOUR BUSINESS

When it comes to marketing your business, there are several steps you need to take. First, establish a target market, then define your brand. Then, after you've developed a plan, you need to put it into practice to effectively market your business. Let's look at the steps you need to take and see how you can effectively market your business from all aspects.

TARGET MARKET

The target market for your pet hotel will obviously consist

of pet owners in a specific geographic area. You are limited to those who can both afford to travel and pay the fees for a pet to stay with you. When you are considering your geographical area, you should conduct thorough research in order to find areas that aren't saturated with similar services and focus your marketing on the services you offer that allow you to meet community needs.

DEFINE YOUR BRAND

Once you have a target market in mind, you need to focus on defining your brand. Your brand is a way to identify what your company stands for and how your business is viewed by the public. Having a well-defined brand will help you stand out from the competition. Then you can focus your marketing on endeavors that benefit your business.

HOW TO FOCUS YOUR MARKETING

The key to focusing your marketing is to focus on the marketing system you are using and the goals you want to achieve. The first thing you need is a strong marketing plan. This is an important thing; otherwise, you are simply relying on what you hope to work. Without a plan, you are simply trying various marketing efforts, which can either lead to success or cause you to lose a lot.

With most marketing efforts being digitally focused today, most marketing is low-cost. However, it will require time and planning to be successful. Therefore, your focus should be on building a large email list of both prospects and, if you have them, existing customers. It is important to split your list between these two.

Another thing you need to focus on is building a strong social media presence for your business. This includes popular platforms such as Facebook, Twitter, Instagram, and Pinterest, as well as any other places where your prospects and customers may be. Social media allows you to access tools to market your services strategically in a way that is worth your time.

The majority of your social media posts should focus on high-quality information that prospects and clients can use to improve their lives with pets, pet-related entertainment, or to highlight ways to provide quality, fun daily care for pets. This will help establish a stage for strategic service marketing posts that we'll discuss in a moment.

EXAMINE FINANCIAL REPORTS

Financial reports are a reality of owning a business and are key to maximizing profits. There is one key financial report and three performance measures you need to consider when strategizing your marketing. Your bookkeeper can provide this information, but you need to know how to quickly review the reports and what to do with them.

The most important report to consider is the monthly Profit and Loss Statement. However, just reviewing these numbers from the last month is nothing more than looking at history. To improve future results, you need a Profit and Loss Statement from your bookkeeper that compares actual results to your budget. If you don't have a budget established, then you should compare last month's results to the same month from the prior year. However, it is highly recommended that you have an established budget. It is also important that you split your income by the key services you provide in each Profit and Loss Statement.

The three key performance measures that you need to review for your business each month are the following:

> Occupancy for all key services (such as boarding, grooming, etc.)
>
> Number of pet visits for each service (such as grooming, training, etc.)
>
> Revenue per pet (or total revenue by service divided by visits)

These reports should be a part of your monthly strategy session. You should hold a strategy meeting in the first two weeks of the month to set a deadline for your bookkeeper to finish all bookkeeping tasks by the end of the month.

It is important to have your strategy meeting away from the business and to power off your phone. As a business owner, you need uninterrupted hours in order to find a way to maximize your business profits. It is also a great time for your staff and employees to learn to make small decisions on their own.

THE STRATEGY SESSION

Start the session by reviewing your Profit and Loss Statement. Note which service areas performed better than the budget or better than the previous year. If you know the reason, then make a note on the report.

Next, you need to review the income areas that were below budget or less than the previous year. Again, you should note down any noted reasons. If you don't know the reason, then add it to a "to-do" list to figure out. If you aren't sure how to do an analysis, then make sure you ask an accountant to help you.

The next step is to look at your revenue per pet data for each service area. Ask yourself how closely they match your full-price rate per service. If there is a major difference, then you should make an analysis of your discount programs a high priority on your "to-do" list. You can also ask an accountant to help you calculate your profitability for an individual service area.

Now is the time to review your occupancy numbers for each service. Is there an area where you can increase sales? Do you feel the current occupancy numbers will repeat in the next month or even in the next three months? If you answered yes, then this service is one you want to target in your short-term marketing plan, especially if it was short of the budget.

Focus on this service within your current monthly email communication and social media posts. Make sure your clients know you offer the service, and consider offering an incentive to prospects and/or existing clients to try it. You may even want to consider creating separate offers for prospects and existing clients. Just make sure you have a segmented list that is easy to customize for each group.

The great thing about social media is that you can provide incentives, such as a fun contest. It also allows you to control the amount of free or discounted services you offer.

It may make financial sense to offer short-term discounts to many clients, but make sure you know the service will still generate profits.

When you have a marketing strategy session in the following month, you want to first determine if your targeted marketing campaign was successful. Ask yourself, did your income and occupancy for the target service increase? Did you also see an increase in business profits? If the answer is yes, then you can celebrate. Repeat the review process and consider choosing a different service for the month or try a different incentive for the same service a second month in a row.

When you combine financial results with a marketing system, you will be able to increase business profits. Prioritize this time to work on your business rather than in your business. You'll definitely see improved profits. So now, let us consider your marketing options for putting these results to work for you.

Marketing Options

Pet ownership is on the rise, and a recent Forbes report shows that millennials are at the front of the pack. As this demand increases, so do the competitors for your pet hotel business. Whether you own a pet hotel or offer additional services such as grooming, daycare, or retail sales, it can be difficult to stand out from the competition.

Many consumers use the internet today to find, research and hire services. This means your online presence and reputation are extremely important. Let's look at the top marketing ideas that can help you to grow your pet hotel business and stand out from the competition.

Building an Online Presence

The internet's ability to grow a business is very important. Therefore, it is important to have a mobile-friendly, responsive website, as it is essentially your business's online office. The website is where potential customers will find your services among your competitors. The website is also a valuable resource for existing customers who want to interact with your pet hotel. To build a strong website and online presence, you need to take 10 steps.

CREATE A WEBSITE

At one time, having a quality outdoor sign or storefront was the way to attract business. Today, having a well-designed website can help a business attract customers and showcase its professionalism. Your website is open 24/7, even when your business isn't. Even when you can't answer a phone or talk to customers, they can get answers to their most common questions on your website. This saves everyone time and provides a way to consistently attract attention to your business.

CREATE A SOCIAL MEDIA PRESENCE

Having a social media presence and a blog offers several benefits to your business. Both of these mediums allow you to connect with your customers directly.

Blog posts are a way for you to discuss specific topics in-depth. Blog posts can address key searches for pet care, health, and related topics, helping your site rank higher in search results and attract new visitors.

Social platforms such as Facebook, Twitter, and Instagram are great ways to regularly remind your customers in their feeds. This can help increase the chance of repeat visits. Having a social profile also allows you to chat directly with your customers to answer questions, resolve concerns, or help unhappy customers.

Local SEO Optimization

For many pet-related businesses, it isn't how your company ranks on a global scale but rather how you rank in your city or other regional areas. This is why it is important that you optimize your business to rank highest in the location of your pet hotel. A major issue for many businesses is inaccuracies in NAP (Name, Address, and Phone Number). If your business name is on Yelp but listed under a different name in the Yellow Pages, this can confuse Google and decrease your website rankings. Local search engine optimization is a great way to increase your online presence with those who are directly looking for the services you offer.

Develop a Referral System

Referrals often turn out to be your best customers. This is because people trust others who refer them to a business. It is easy to build a referral system; you just need to ask customers to provide feedback on your company. Then ask those who leave positive reviews to share their feedback online so others can see it. If there is negative feedback, you can handle their concerns offline and, hopefully, turn them into a happy customer who will leave a positive review online.

Asking for Reviews

Getting feedback from customers is an excellent way to better understand your clients and ensure you are meeting their needs. One of the easiest and best ways to get feedback is to simply ask for feedback, but can you do the same with reviews? Let's consider three main ways that you can ask for reviews from clients.

Learning How to Ask

You can quickly get feedback from existing clients by simply asking them. You can simply print this request on the receipt or ask online once the checkout process is complete. While you may feel that asking is too forward, statistics show that 7 out of 10 customers will write a review of a business if asked.

Become Creative

There are a few different ways you can ask customers for feedback without coming off as too aggressive. If your software has a survey feature, then you can follow up automatically. There are also software programs that allow you to reach out to customers via text or email, making it easier for them to write positive reviews and ensuring they are posted in the right places.

Learn From What Doesn't Work

Online reviews are a great way to improve your business, but getting them the wrong way can actually be a bad thing. When asking for reviews, it is important that you avoid the following:

Buying fake reviews from those who aren't actual clients

Bribing clients in order to get positive reviews

Spamming clients with review requests

While the above may seem like a good idea at times, they won't provide genuine reviews for a business. Google and Yelp are improving at catching fake or forced reviews; companies are penalized when they are removed from their platforms. Potential clients are also likely to see through these reviews and choose your competitors for their pet boarding needs.

PAID ADVERTISING AND FACEBOOK ADS

There are two ways you can have an online presence. One is by showing up organically through SEO, and the other is by paying for ads. Investing time and energy into SEO can provide long-term results. On the other hand, paid advertisements allow you to get noticed right away. Just remember that your results will often stop the moment you stop paying for advertising. If you have extra budget for marketing, this can be a great way to quickly gain visibility across several platforms and increase your online presence.

Facebook is one of the most popular platforms for animal lovers, making it a great place to target your audience. There are several types of Facebook ads to choose from, including video, image, and carousel ads with multiple images. These ads can be used for branding or even to generate leads by adding a form directly to the ad. Different from Google Search Ads, Facebook Ads allow you to target your marketing based on age, income, and interests.

GOOGLE ADVERTISING

This advertising method will leverage Google's popularity. Nearly 70% of all internet searches are handled by Google. Google Ads come up when someone searches for pet care services. These ads come from keywords and can be filtered to show only when people near your location search for terms related to your business.

Retargeting to Improve Traffic

This option can be useful if someone visits your website but doesn't sign up for your services. Using cookies, you can target these website visitors with advertisements when they visit other websites. These are known as Retargeting Ads because you are focusing on people who have already visited your website, making them more likely to use your services.

In addition to knowing your marketing options, it is important to know how to use them during slow seasons to improve your profits.

How to Use Marketing in the Slow Seasons

Pet boarding is an on-and-off business that depends on the time of year. There are times when your hotel is going to be so booked that you won't be able to take reservations for months. But during other times of the year, you may be so deserted that the facility will actually be quiet. During these slower periods, you need to get creative about finding pets to bring into your facility. Sometimes this means offering other services other than boarding. Consider the following ideas to market your business and keep customers coming, even during the slow seasons.

FUN IN THE OFF-SEASON

Make sure you celebrate all the small holidays. Have fun pet activities that revolve around all the quieter national holidays. Just a few ideas include St. Patrick's Day, Earth Day and Valentine's Day. The events don't have to be big, but something as simple as a themed puppy party. Nothing is more fun for a customer than an event where they can take their pets.

You can even create your own holidays to host themed events. The larger holidays will keep you busy, so you should create events for smaller holidays related to pets. These are becoming increasingly popular. Consider the following options:

National Train Your Dog Month in January

Love Your Pet Day on February 20th

National Dog Biscuit Day on February 23rd

National Kids and Pets Day on April 26th

National Dog Day on August 26th

The list is endless, and you can easily control how many holidays your business promotes each month.

THEMED PARTIES

When you plan a themed pet party, make sure you get artistic. Invite pet owners to create pet art. Some of the art will turn out quite attractive. You can even frame some of the works in your lobby. Owners will enjoy the chance to display their pet's artwork.

Dress Up Nights

Nearly everyone has dressed up their pets at some point. You can celebrate this by having a dress-up and photography event. You can get creative and have the owners dress up as well. Have contests with prizes and post the results on your social media.

Pet and People Mixers

This is a great option if you offer daycare and have pets that are well socialized with others. Some great mixer options include birthday parties, breed-specific clubs, puppy parties, and groups. There are plenty of things you can think up. You can even consider pet-friendly food and treat tasting events. Invite owners to bring their pets to these events. It can also be a great way to increase retail sales as well.

Spa and Grooming Services

Pet grooming services are a great way to keep customers coming to your pet hotel every six to eight weeks. If you don't offer a full grooming service, you can still charge clients extra for a bath. Offering bathing services can be a great way to send your clients home with a clean pet, but it can also help keep people returning to your facility, even between boarding visits. Perhaps you can offer things like a yearly bathing club card or a buy-4-get-1-free bathing deal to get people to come more often. Even if you don't offer grooming services, you can still offer additional spa services to pamper pets. If you can't offer any of these services daily, you can still host a party once a month to offer them.

SPORTING EVENTS FOR COMPETITIVE PETS

Consider building a pet playground. Have a membership so people can use this area year-round. You can even have an agility course and tunnels for an interactive experience. If you are near a water source, you can build a water dock and charge a membership fee for access during the warm months. You can even get help building some of these projects by offering sponsorships to local businesses so they can display their banner on the side of your facilities, promoting their business.

You can start various pet sports leagues, such as Frisbee or ball clubs. Once these teams have enough members regularly, you can even consider hosting spectator events and championships. This gives you a great way to increase income while also advertising your business.

You can also create a private dog show with interactive judging and awards. This will be great for the everyday person who wants to show off their pet but doesn't want to compete professionally.

Perhaps you can consider a talent show for animals. You can even offer services to help teach pets before the show. There is no limit to the things pets can learn to do. When promoted effectively, this type of event is a great way to attract new clients, as it can also draw people from outside the community.

USE THE INTERNET

It is important to have a website, as we've already discussed. Make sure the website lists who you are, what you do, and why people should choose you over the competition. You can also choose to join an online pet boarding reservation service. Ensure your business is listed on all major search engines.

EXPAND BEYOND ON-SITE SERVICES

Consider offering at-home services such as dog walking and pet sitting. There are also ancillary services such as pet food delivery, plant watering, mail pickup and more. Taking care of pets while owners are away doesn't have to just occur in your pet hotel.

ENSURE YOU'RE MAKING A PROFIT

While there will be expenses associated with the above ideas, the goal is to ensure you make a profit at the end of the month. Whether this is through the charge of participation or from membership fees. Carefully plan the costs of your events for the month or year, then adjust your prices accordingly. Offering yearly passes is a great way to get upfront revenue to cover costs throughout the year and also gives you an advance on the money you need to plan monthly events.

While we've already discussed the use of a website, let's also look closer at how a website can help you in your marketing endeavors.

How to Use Your Website for Marketing

More and more people are turning to the internet to find pet care experts. This is why having a strong web presence is key to meeting your revenue goals. With today's economy in the midst of COVID, the number of potential clients is declining, and people are becoming more selective. People are sure to check out websites before deciding whom to call. Consider the following ten things you can do to improve your web marketing.

Own Your Web Address

Known more formally as a URL (uniform resource locator) or domain name. This is your business's address on the Internet. Many website companies will register a web address with your name, but retain ownership of it. If you don't register the website yourself, then you should check with your web designer or web marketing provider for help.

Display Professional Association Logos

When potential clients visit your website, you should quickly convey your credibility through top-tier association logos on your home page. This conveys that you provide a premium, professional service. If you already have a logo on your website, then make sure it is the most up-to-date version. Outdated, sloppy graphics make your business look the same.

Check Your Web Design Standards

Make sure your website doesn't have any "old school" web design standards. Scrolling text, animated graphics, sound effects, and site visit counters all show that you aren't keeping up with the times. Clear, clean displays of both text and animations that support overall marketing messages are the newest thing.

Easy Phone Number

How easy is it for visitors to your website to find your phone number? Contact information needs to be clearly accessible from the home page and in the website's navigation. It is best to have your phone number and physical address in the upper right-hand corner of the main header. No matter where your visitor goes within the website, your phone number and general service area will be visible. People will easily move on to the competition if it is too difficult to reach your business.

Review Your Website

Take a look through your website right now and make sure there is no outdated information or misspelled words. Either of these mistakes will cause your business to look bad. Make sure you take the time to review your website every six months. Look for broken links, missing images, and text that is appropriate and up to date. Site reviews are something many business owners overlook, but should be just as important as physical property maintenance. Make sure all pages are finished and that everything comes across as professional.

INCLUDE A BUSINESS LOGO

The logo for your business should be in the header at the top of your website. The logo should look crisp online. Ask your web or logo designer to create a logo version that is optimized for the website. Internet users today are experts at distinguishing between businesses that look like pros online and those that aren't. A graphic that used to look good may not appear the same to the newer generation of potential clients.

ADD PHOTOS

Photos are a way to bring your website to life. People want to see a face to the business. Photos help people connect to your business. Depending on the layout of your website, the ideal place for photos is on the home page, the Contact Us page, and the About Us page.

PROFESSIONAL ASSOCIATION CONTENT

If you are a member of a professional association, then ask if they have content for members to use online. Call or email to see what's available. Affiliates are often a good source of content for FAQ pages and for the copy that showcases your value to potential clients.

Remove Irrelevant Information

Make sure you remove anything from your website that isn't relevant. Visitor counters, web search forms, and time and temperature displays are all sources of distracting clutter and should be removed to avoid an outdated feel. Remember to keep your site clear and focused on the services you offer.

Highlight Seasonal Services

Based on the season, make sure you adjust your website to highlight seasonal services. The mission of your website is to deliver key, compelling information. This makes it more compelling to interested clients. Just make sure the information is seasonally appropriate.

In addition to these tips for creating a strong website, you also need to know how to improve your website's online presence.

IMPROVING YOUR WEB PRESENCE

Your online image and presence are everything these days. This is where you can make yourself look big. The following are seven tips to help you build and maintain a successful online presence.

SHORTEN HOME PAGE CONTENT

Website visitors don't want to be overwhelmed by long paragraphs that read like an essay on the home page. They also don't want endless details and paragraphs on service description pages. If your visitors feel overloaded, they will either leave the website or, at the very least, be left without a strong reason to call you and use your services. Therefore, your website information should be concise and clear. You should describe your services in short sentences or using bullet points. Scan your homepage in 15 seconds and ask yourself: Does it clearly state who you are, what sets you apart from the competition, and which areas you serve?

ADD PHOTOS AND VIDEOS

Photos of your facility and staff will help add a personal touch to your web presence and distinguish you from the competition. Videos can also be a great way to engage with potential clients and keep their attention long enough to spread your message.

DON'T DIVERT, CONVERT

Your focus should be on converting website visitors into leads. Many business owners focus on design details rather than on the basic task of generating business. Consider your home page: Do you see your phone number and service area at first glance? If you don't have this information readily visible, you are missing the most important element of your website for converting leads. If you want to generate clients, then you need a phone number that is easy to find.

GOOGLE PLACES

It is important that you go to Google Places and do three

things: find, claim and fully complete your business profile listing. These are free and key to getting your business noticed when people search for the services you offer. When complete, these profile pages will give you an edge over the competition and help you reach more potential clients.

These profiles are organized and displayed in a way that makes it easy for searchers to move from one to another. Your business can appear better than the competition by having a complete profile that lists all the areas you serve, service descriptions, and photos of your facility and/or staff.

WEB ANALYTICS

Most people visit a website to view the home page, services page, and maybe the contact or about us pages. You can create better content and generate more leads if you have a better understanding of people's on-site behavior. You can learn this by looking at web analytics.

ONLINE REVIEWS

Customers rank your business from one to five stars on leading search engines and local directory sites. They can also include comments on their experience with you. Focus on getting your best customers to post reviews on top sites. At the very least, your online marketing strategy needs to include an understanding of how online rating sites work.

BOLD DESIGN CHANGE

Change can be a good thing. When building or overhauling your website, consider using a bold element that appears on your home page. Consider a textured background or a consistent photo that appears on each page.

When it comes to first-time website design, the best option is to be conservative. If your business has grown and your image is more distinct, then you can consider a new design element for your website. Consider the following ideas:

A large-scale, stunning photo on the home page

A single, bold color that links to your logo

A landing page with a company name, tagline, and phone number

A web video on the homepage

All of these things can help you attract the attention of potential clients. It is important to be bold but careful. Don't cause the customer to get distracted or overloaded; otherwise, you'll be doing your business a disservice.

How to Use Facebook for Marketing

In a crowded market such as the pet industry, it is important to set yourself apart from your competition. The best way to do this is through a simple video marketing tool called Facebook Live.

Facebook Live is an easy-to-use feature you can access from the Facebook app on your phone. With nothing more than the touch of a button, you can "go live" and talk directly to your targeted audience on Facebook. People can ask questions in real-time. Also, it will stay on your feed after you've finished, so people can still see the video even if they missed it when you were live.

Best of all, it requires no tech skills, and the video will feel more personal than a Facebook post. This tool allows you to easily build the power tool of the like/know/trust factor that potential clients need.

While the following information applies to any video, there are additional benefits to using Facebook Live. One of these benefits is that you can get an extra boost from the Facebook algorithm, and more followers will see it. There are nearly 100 million Internet users who watch live videos every day. This clearly shows an increasing demand for live video. Consider the following statistics:

> Social media provides 1200% more shares than both images and texts combined

> Businesses that use videos have an average 41% increase in web traffic

Facebook Live video watchers will watch three times longer than non-live videos

Consider the following ten ideas for your next Facebook Live video:

TOUR THE FACILITY

You likely give tours to potential clients when they first visit your facility, but why not offer one virtually? This allows all your Facebook followers to see what your facility looks like and might even get those few potential clients who are on the bubble to sign up for your services. This can also be a great way to introduce yourself and show people who will be caring for their pets.

INTRODUCE STAFF MEMBERS

Offering a short introduction and a video of your staff is a great way to make people feel comfortable when they leave their pets with you. Just remember to keep it simple, perhaps introducing a staff member of the week.

Offer a Q&A Session

Do you have frequent questions that clients always ask? Make a list of these questions and then answer them live on camera. There are plenty of things to keep you busy for several videos.

Introduce Pets

Cats and dogs are very popular on the Internet, so this means you have a great resource. Introduce unique pets in your care; just make sure you have proper consent from the owners first.

Go Behind the Scenes

Many people see the front and customer sides of your business, but many may not know what goes into the daily operations of a pet hotel. Take your audience through a part of your typical day. Perhaps showcase special activities you do with your guests. This can demonstrate the value of the services you offer your clients.

Highlight Accomplishments

If you attend a seminar or conference, consider going Live and sharing what you've learned. This shows your dedication to benefiting both your facility, industry, and the pets in your care.

Recommend Other Businesses

Do you always make the same recommendation to clients who ask for related services such as grooming? Then consider going live with a video that recommends these other businesses. Perhaps these businesses will then return the favor and do the same for you.

Review Top Toys

Do you have products or toys that are most popular with your charges? During the holidays, there are always many articles and lists online about top toys, treats, and other items. You can go one step further by showing, on camera, how well these items work with animals. It can even potentially increase retail sales.

Offer Pet Care Tips

As a member of the pet industry, you are considered an expert. You can share tips that people may find valuable. These can be things like safe ways to clean a dog's ears to tips for pilling a cat. This will increase people's confidence when leaving pets in your care.

Introducing Satisfied Clients

Perhaps you have a loyal client that you really enjoy. Ask them if they are willing to do a review live on camera. This is a great way to get referrals.

These ideas are easy to implement with the Facebook app on your phone. The first few times may be awkward, but just consider them practice and keep trying. Soon it will be second nature, and you'll be enjoying the rewards that come from these videos.

Choose a schedule that works for you. Do a Facebook Live video once a week or once a day; it is ultimately up to you and what you can achieve. However, the key is consistency. If you want quick growth, you should do them daily, or at least every other day, for three to four weeks. Then you can drop down to twice a week. If you already have a waitlist, once a week can keep you at the forefront of people's minds.

Facebook Live videos are the fastest and most cost-effective way to make yourself stand out from the competition. You will know this marketing method is working when you are getting more messages and find yourself being recognized in the local community.

How to Use Retention Marketing to Keep Clients

Retaining just 5% of customers will increase your profits by 25-125%. Increasing client retention by just two percent is the same financial impact as cutting costs by ten percent. Since getting new clients is an endeavor, it makes sense that you want to do what you can to keep them.

If you are having trouble establishing a marketing plan,

then perhaps you should consider retention marketing first, since it can be a bit easier. Unlike public and referral marketing for new clients, retention marketing focuses on honoring and strengthening relationships with your existing clients. You don't have to worry about being rejected since you are marketing to people who are already using your services.

Benefits of Retention Marketing

Consider the following reasons why you should consider retention marketing:

> It will help you retain clients during financial hard times, such as recessions, rate increases, and market volatility.

> It will help you educate clients to better understand dogs and their behavior.

> It helps maintain brand loyalty and presence, making you less likely to lose clients to the competition.

To get new clients, you'll need to stay within the field of view of existing clients, so they are more likely to tell others about you.

Next, let's consider some retention marketing ideas. Consider the ones that best fit your budget, skills, and interests. Just remember that the more marketing endeavors you can do, the better your results.

STAY IN TOUCH

Make sure your clients aren't only hearing from you when there is an issue. Regular communication with clients can provide a buffer should you need to deliver bad news. If you offer a service that takes place away from client supervision, it's important to find regular ways to show clients what you do. Report cards for pets are fun and share progress. If you are boarding animals, then send a quick text message or email each day to share something about the pets in your care.

Education

A great way to educate clients and keep in touch is through an e-newsletter. There are services such as Constant Contact and Mailchimp that can help you send professional monthly newsletters. Just remember to keep these short: limit it to one useful or entertaining article, a client dog profile, and/or a brief sales update. You can also partner with a local trainer to do a free talk for clients. This can help provide exposure for both businesses.

Say Thank You

Consider offering small discounts to repeat customers. If you offer different services, then perhaps you can offer a discount if a client uses more than one. For example, daycare clients may get a discounted fee for onboarding. Just make sure you are careful when discounting ongoing services since this can lead to a loss of profits. Make sure you reinforce referrals by offering a small discount. Perhaps something like ten percent off a booking if they refer a client.

Be Social

When it comes to retention marketing, social media is the ideal tool. There are many social media options to choose from. As we have seen, Facebook is a great tool for pet businesses. However, don't forget about things like Pinterest and Instagram as well. These social media options are quickly gaining traction. Both of these sites are image-based, and you are sure to have a number of great photos to share. If you or staff members are in the habit of recording short videos, then Instagram can be a great tool.

However, socializing doesn't have to limit you to the Internet. You can also find creative ways to get clients together with you and other clients. As we've discussed before, there are plenty of ways to have fun events that attract people and their pets.

Focus on nurturing and deepening client relationships to help strengthen your business, educate owners and even have a little fun on the side. Retention marketing is key to improving your bottom line.

DAILY OPERATIONAL CONSIDERATIONS

Once you are in the final stages of opening your business or after you've opened your doors, you need to start focusing on your day-to-day operations. Once you're open for business, there are quite a few things you need to keep in mind to have a successful business that continues to grow. First, let's look at the health and safety of your business and those in your care.

HEALTH AND SAFETY

When it comes to health and safety, there is a lot that you can do to improve your day-to-day operations. The first thing you need to do is consider your design. If you haven't already opened your business, this is still a chance to make changes. So let's consider how design can help you improve health and safety.

How Design Helps

The design of a pet hotel facility can help make cleaning easier. Design troubles can sometimes be minor and just need a simple fix. However, other times, design mistakes can take their toll on a building after years of use. Often, the troubles of a building design come down to one of the following areas:

    Water

    Drainage

    Air Quality

Mold Growth

Cleaning

The consistent cleaning needed in a pet facility can be tough on the building. If not handled properly, water will easily find its way into walls and other areas, promoting mold growth and/or causing serious structural damage. Owning a pet hotel is a lot of work, and there is no such thing as a self-cleaning kennel. However, with a proper design, you can make cleaning much easier. When you eliminate the cleaning water from the building right away, you'll reduce the risk of mold growth and rust. It also helps to keep the air in the building free of moisture.

Beyond design, it is important to have a clear, robust health and safety program. Let's consider how you can create one of these.

CREATING A HEALTH AND SAFETY PROGRAM

The best asset to a pet hotel is the employees. While not legally required, you should be fully committed to creating a health and safety program. Safety is not only your responsibility but also the focus of each employee. Therefore, you should prioritize staff involvement in complying with a health and safety program. You need to ask yourself how you adequately convey the key elements of a good program through things like knowledge, control, support, and training. This allows employees to be fully equipped to ensure they aren't putting people at risk and to make appropriate changes.

A successful health and safety program is achieved by doing more than simply asking employees to comply. Rather, you need to offer proper training, education, resources and authority so the staff can take on the safety process and fully invest their time in the program. One of the most effective ways is to have a Safety Committee of both staff and management, who can review safety procedures and real-world accidents. The best program is proactive rather than reactive. Don't wait until the worst happens before you make safety a priority in your business.

There are several key elements that need to be integrated into a successful health and safety program. Let's consider several of them.

Having a written Safety Program details the proper procedures and conduct needed to ensure a safe working environment. The details should include items such as expectations, consequences or corrective actions as established by management.

Along with this written program, you should conduct a safety orientation before each employee receives their first job assignment. This allows new employees to be aware of any hazards in the work environment and ensures there is a clear set of rules for minimizing hazards. Doing a walk-around with employees in an assigned area is an essential part of this process. After new employees have completed the safety training, there should be a signed acknowledgment.

A Job Safety Analysis (JSA) allows you to carefully study and record each step of a job. Through this, you can identify existing or potential job hazards from a health and safety perspective. This allows you to develop the proper way for employees to perform their jobs to reduce or eliminate hazards. When you conduct a JSA, you should also consider accident frequency, severity and repetitive exposure.

The key to a successful health and safety program is training. While there are many laws governing employee safety training, even without legal mandates, you should still focus on periodic safety training. This will help lessen injuries and ultimately protect your bottom-line profit. While training topics are important, some are required by law and/or vital to implementing preventive measures. These include the following:

    Hazard Communication

    Personal Protective Equipment

    Emergency Action Plan

    Bloodborne Pathogens

Some additional training areas that you may want to consider going over and/or implementing include the following:

    Proper Recordkeeping

Lock-Out/Tag-Out

Slip, Trip and Fall Protection

Proper Lifting

CPR/First Aid/AED

Proper Machine Operation

Ladder Safety

Ergonomic Analysis

These are just a few key areas; you may have others that are important for your location or specific to the services your pet hotel offers.

To prevent future incidents, accident investigation is another important tool. Employees should be required to report any accident immediately. The resulting investigation should ideally be conducted by an immediate supervisor as soon as they learn of the incident, and all required forms should be completed. Accidents should then be reviewed by the Safety Committee to see if any action is needed to prevent further occurrences.

Having a Return to Work Program will reduce the amount of time an employee is away from work. It will also show employees they are completely cared about by you. This program should ideally include detailed job descriptions for all business functions. If an employee goes to the doctor, then this program allows the physician to know what the employees are expected to do as a part of their job. The physician can then determine what, if any, functions the employee can do.

In addition, management should try to provide light duty options for the physician to consider when determining the work status of an employee. If you immediately think that you have no light duty, then you need to open your mind a little more. Any task that can be approved for light-duty will prevent the employee from staying home and being non-productive. The department in charge of handling claims should monitor the status of the employee's work and keep the supervisor informed.

Do you think you're ready for anything? If you have insurance, you're covered. But are you sure? There are a few things you need to consider when developing an Emergency Preparedness Program:

Bomb Threats

Cyber Attack

Emergency Contact List

Evacuation Routes

Robberies

Toxic Chemical Releases

Utility Outage

Violence in the Workplace

Weather Emergencies

All of the above will require planning, training and drilling to ensure complete success if and when it needs to be implemented. If you aren't proactive, then it will be too late when something happens, and this could potentially put your business in peril. Therefore, you should also consider creating a partnership with local agencies that may respond in the event of an emergency to reduce some of the stress you'll face when one of the above occurs. Make sure you also include your employees in the planning process so they will feel like a part of the program.

These are just a few of the most important aspects of a health and safety program. It is important to remember that the new employees don't know anything about your operation when they first start working with you. Therefore, this program is important and needs to be successful to lessen risk and direct impact on your bottom-line profits. Orientation and training for your health and safety program are a priority, since putting safety first means you'll be able to avoid the worst. Let's look a little more closely at the most important item on this list.

HAVING AN EMERGENCY PREPAREDNESS PLAN

We've all seen coverage of major natural disasters on the news. The aftermath of these disasters lasts for weeks, months and in some cases, even years. Many pet care businesses haven't made a plan for what they will do if their area is affected by a natural disaster. How do you keep the pets in your care safe and ensure they are well cared for? The big disasters are obvious, but have you considered the small emergencies that affect your business, such as a fire or a hazardous materials spill?

Emergency preparedness is important for saving the lives of the pets in your care and for helping others who may not be prepared for major events. Prevention measures also ensure that you protect valuable business information and keep your business up and running. It can also reduce losses of equipment, revenue and inventory.

Advanced planning can provide both clients and employees with a sense of security and loyalty. They know that the care and protection of their pets is first at your business.

DEFINING AN EMERGENCY

A facility emergency is defined as any unplanned event that could cause significant injury or death to pets, employees, clients or the public. These events can also disrupt operations, shut down the business or cause physical and/or environmental damage. Consider some common emergencies that can affect your business:

- Fire

- Flood

- Gas Leak

- Hurricane

- Tornado

- Earthquake

Power Outage

Burglary

Riot

Mudslide

Avalanche

Lightning Strike

Volcanic Eruption

Oil/Fuel/Chemical/Sewage Spill

Wildfire

Excessive Snow

Nuclear Hazards

TALK WITH YOUR INSURANCE AGENT

Your insurance agent is a great resource for recommendations on fire prevention and other protective measures. If your area is prone to flooding, you should understand the risks and consider getting flood insurance. You shouldn't wait until an emergency occurs to find out if you are properly insured. Rather, you should take the time to call or meet with your agent and review your policy to determine whether you are adequately covered. Agents can also provide you with suggestions on how to protect your business and reduce your insurance premiums.

INTERNAL RESOURCES

All pet care businesses have necessary components such as fire protection, communications equipment, first-aid supplies, warning devices and emergency generators. For employees, you want to have an emergency operations center where they can report during a problem. There should also be a supply of food, water, blankets, flashlights and other emergency supplies in case staff have to stay over during a disaster. There should also be a backup plan for computer systems, files and essential equipment. You should also consider your backup equipment, such as water pumps and a generator.

OUTSIDE HELP

During an emergency, other services and businesses may need assistance from external resources. Make sure you get their phone numbers and reach out to them in advance so they can prepare if and when they are needed. Your emergency call list should include the following:

- Local emergency management office
- Fire department
- Hazardous materials response team
- EMS
- Hospitals
- Local veterinarians

Local and state police

Community service organizations

Contractors

Suppliers of emergency equipment

You should also know whether your community has plans in place in the event of an emergency. Also, know if there is an established evacuation route should you need to leave the area.

STAFF TRAINING

Proper training for the staff is an important part of being prepared for an emergency. Your staff needs to be taught how to report an emergency to the proper authorities, how to use an alarm system and how to identify the need to shut off gas, electricity and water. Staff drills should be conducted for different emergency situations. Have a meeting place and a check-in procedure to confirm everyone's safety. You should also have an established procedure to warn pet owners and employees who aren't on the premises in the event of an emergency.

Review the Facility and Grounds

It is important to know your facility and the grounds around it. You should ensure your facility complies with all applicable safety and construction codes. When local resources respond to your emergency, you will need building and site maps. Some important things to document are the location of utilities and shutoffs, floor plans, fire extinguisher locations, exits, stairways and hazardous materials.

Ensure you have the proper monitoring systems and that they are tested regularly. Are there modifications to your building that can protect your facility, such as waterproofing or seismic engineering enhancements? You should identify and label outside containers and emergency shelters if needed.

EMERGENCY RESPONSE ELEMENTS

During an emergency, it is important to warn, update and notify employees and clients. You will need to develop your own communication system. Consider the following implementation ideas:

Make an announcement to everyone in the building

Call the staff who isn't on the premises at the time

Put announcements or updates on the voice mail system

Place announcements on social media and your website

Evacuated pets should be notified at emergency numbers

Evacuation Procedures and Operational Shut Down

In extreme situations, you may need to shut down operations for people's safety and/or evacuate the facility. If this occurs, it is important to have a developed plan and guidelines in place. This should include something like the following:

> Have a predetermined staff meeting location to account for everyone

> Call 911 or other emergency numbers

> Have a source for weather alerts or other updates

> Remove pets as safety conditions allow

> Assure computer files are backed up off-premises or remove the backup

> Shut off gas lines if appropriate

Turn off electricity and water supplies if appropriate

Have easy access to emergency supplies and first aid kits

Close all windows and doors

If you can't move pets off-premises, move them to a safe area of the facility

Move vehicles to a safe location and ensure they are filled with fuel

Since some emergencies will require evacuation, specific details will need to be outlined. For example, you will need to determine ahead of time how pets will be removed if needed, where they will be taken, who will be responsible and how they will be cared for when moved.

PROTECTING VITAL RECORDS

This is one of the most important things in an emergency.

It will ensure your business's viability after an emergency. A copy of all records should be stored off-site so you can access pet and client information in the event of an on-site emergency.

Restoring Operations and Assessing Damage

Restoring operations after an emergency needs to happen quickly as long as the area is safe. There should be a list of items needed for restoration. This list should include utilities, computers and alarms. If there is any damage, then you should make a written assessment, take pictures or video and contact your insurance company right away. Water should also be tested before use since it can be contaminated. Pets should only be moved back into the building once it is safe. If possible, you may need to reach out to see if other shelters can offer aid, or you can offer assistance to other places that may not be as prepared as you.

Implementation

Just writing out an emergency plan doesn't mean it will

be implemented. Once you have a plan, make sure you communicate it to your staff. It is important that everyone gets the details of what might be involved. Don't simply write a plan and put it in a drawer. Rather, you want to review it periodically, make updates as needed and make new staff aware.

Writing out procedures and lists are excellent way to be proactive. The procedures and lists may change as your business grows, so you need to check and update them at least annually.

There are many considerations and scenarios to consider when it comes to possible emergencies. The uniqueness of each facility will inform the development of a detailed plan. The best facilities are those that are proactive and plan for the worst-case scenarios. Clients depend on you for quality care, and being prepared is a great way to earn their trust.

Another important part of your day-to-day operations is your employees. The first thing you need to consider is hiring your employees.

HIRING EMPLOYEES

When you initially start your pet hotel, you may be able to run the business on your own for a little while. However, as your business grows, you may need to hire additional help. You will need to make sure you budget for employee salaries as well as related expenses such as workman's comp insurance, paid time off and health insurance contributions. So, let's look at what goes into hiring your first employee.

HIRING YOUR FIRST EMPLOYEE

There is a lot more to hiring an employee than simply finding the right person for the job. You also need to focus on interviewing and training. Once you find the right employee, then you need to consider paying payroll, withholding taxes, reporting and state and federal agencies. Consider these tips to help you when hiring your first employee.

While it is great to find the one person with skills in a variety of areas, it can be hard to find someone who can do a variety of tasks well. Rather than looking for the perfect employee, you should start by making a list of all the tasks you do daily or need help with.

Group similar tasks together and identify the must-haves for a new employee to do. This will help you start a job description so you can more effectively find people who can do what you need done. You may not be able to hire for all of your needed positions right away, but at least you'll have an overview of what people need to take day-to-day operations off your hands so you can focus on the more important items or tasks that you are better qualified to do.

You may even find that you don't need a full-time person for certain positions. You may even find out you are better off outsourcing to a company or hiring a freelancer for certain things.

TRAINING EMPLOYEES

One of the biggest complaints from small business owners is that they can't find employees who want to work or know what they are doing. Some of this can be because you are attracting the wrong candidates, because you haven't defined things as instructed in the above section. But the issue may also be that you haven't adequately explained what you want done.

This is often the result of two primary issues. The first is that you, as the business owner, have done all the tasks from the beginning and are having a hard time letting go. This means you aren't giving the employee the chance to do the job you hired them for and are micromanaging the process, which takes away any time savings.

The second issue is that you have all the details in your head and only tell the employee how to do it once, expecting them to do it perfectly. It is unrealistic to expect someone to remember the details. So don't be frustrated if employees need to keep asking you how to do things.

The best way to have an employee do the job you want them to do is to document the process and create an employee handbook. Write down the steps and, if needed, make a video. This will make the process available to employees whenever they are unsure about the steps. Rather than making them come to you whenever they have a question or guessing how to do things, they will be able to have access to the right information.

THE REAL COST OF AN EMPLOYEE

Doing the math to figure out a new employee's wages is simple enough. If you hire someone at $15 an hour and they work 40 hours a week or 50 hours a year, then this will cost you $30,000. However, what you need to know as a business owner is that an employee costs more than an hourly wage or salary. Consider some of the following additional costs.

Taxes can include payroll taxes, federal income tax and state tax withholding. There are also Social Security and Medicare taxes. Federal and state income taxes are withheld from an employee's paycheck, but as the employer, you need to pay into Social Security and Medicare, collectively known as the Federal Insurance Contributions Act (FICA). This is a mandatory tax. For each employee, you need to pay 6.2% to Social Security and 1.45% to Medicare. For a $ 30,000-a-year employee, this means an additional $2,295 annually beyond wages.

Workers' Compensation Insurance provides medical expenses, lost wages and rehabilitation expenses for employees who are injured on the job. Most states require this for all occupations, and it is an added cost to include. The cost will vary depending on the amount of payroll you pay, the risk level of the work performed, and your business's industry. You should get a quote for this before you hire a new employee.

You also need to consider the cost of employee benefits such as health insurance, retirement and other voluntary payroll deductions.

Miscellaneous costs can include things like employee benefits, uniforms, training, supplies and more. These costs all need to be factored into the budget.

All of these costs will add up, and you should figure them out now before you invest in long-term hiring.

EMPLOYER RESPONSIBILITIES

When you hire new employees, there are several new responsibilities to consider. Consider the hiring process, which includes tax registration, filing reports, hanging workplace posters and understanding state and federal regulations. You are now going to have a lot more responsibilities.

Since so much goes into hiring a new employee, it can be a good idea to make sure you clearly know your staffing needs.

DETERMINING STAFFING NEEDS

The National Animal Care and Control Association recommends that animal care locations be staffed each day with the appropriate number of kennel personnel. The appropriate number is the number needed to ensure the facility and all animals within it are maintained at or above minimum care standards.

The formula you should use to determine your staffing needs is your incoming animals per year divided by 365 days, which gives you your incoming animals per day. Then, take the number of animals per day times a four-day holding period to get the number of animals in the shelter per day. Take this number and multiply it by 15 minutes per animal to get the total minutes needed.

Divide this by 60 to get the number of hours needed. Divide by 3 to account for feeding and cleaning hours, and get the number of staff needed per day. This formula is a general guideline, but your individual facility may need more or fewer staff to meet its needs. Once you have the proper number of employees, you need to focus on training them properly.

With careful preparation and proper training, you can onboard new employees at your facility without feeling like you need to hold their hands. Just remember, you need to treat your employees as valued assets you are simply helping to become top achievers. Clients will notice this as well.

As we've already discussed, once you know what the job entails, you can start looking for employees with the right physical, mental and emotional ability. Each facility is unique, so you need to ensure employees can handle what you require of them.

When it comes to hiring employees in the pet care

industry, the solution to finding the right fit is working interviews. After a successful interview, you can require a two-day working interview. This allows new hires to see and fully understand what it is like to work at your facility. This also allows you to gauge whether the employee is a good fit for you.

Once you have hired and trained new employees, your focus needs to switch to retaining good employees.

Retaining Good Employees

Perhaps one of your biggest challenges as a pet hotel owner is to find, motivate and retain quality employees. Studies have shown that employers with an organized, structured approach to employee training are more likely to retain their employees. Retaining quality employees will increase workplace productivity.

Clear communication from the state is the key to a successful relationship between employer and employee. An employee is successful when they know and understand the basic requirements of the position.

One of the more difficult things to instill is a work ethic. Therefore, you want to set high standards for work ethic. Then you can recognize the workers who are responsible and dependable. You should then give them positive and immediate recognition.

Managing a pet hotel goes beyond managing employees. There are a few things you need to do to be an effective pet hotel manager. Let's consider some of these areas.

EFFECTIVE DAILY MANAGEMENT

STREAMLINE YOUR BUSINESS

Perhaps the best use of your time as a pet hotel manager is to streamline your business. You probably started small, but your business may be growing faster than you can keep up with. If you are stressed or short on time, consider improving the following areas to streamline your business.

Set up Processes

The more you can standardize your business, the better. Streamline the intake process so you can easily check-in clients. Have contracts set up on a template. Create a training guide for new employees to quickly get everyone up to speed.

Track Expenses

You will have a range of expenses for your business, as we discussed at the beginning. Tracking your expenses will help you see where your biggest overhead comes from and give you a chance to reduce it.

Use the Right Software

If there is software that can help you do more, then take advantage of it. For example, employee scheduling software can make it easier to track staff schedules. Customer management software helps you to log client preferences and pet allergies. The best software will combine both of these elements and more.

Hire When Needed

When you first start your pet hotel, it won't be long before you realize you are overwhelmed and need help. This is why you should consider hiring employees, either full-time or part-time. Having others help will allow you to focus more on administrative tasks.

Invest in Business Growth

If you reinvest your profits in the company, you can grow your business faster. Insurance is a costly investment, but it will protect you from liability as well as attract new clients who are confident you can protect their animals.

Utilize Effective Marketing Strategies

You are going to need a constant stream of new clients, and the only way you can do this is through effective marketing, as we've already covered. Use the variety of tools we've discussed and have a strong marketing plan in place.

Automate What You Can

Once you've established processes, you should automate as much as possible. When you can avoid doing something manually over and over, you'll save time, and saving time equals saving money.

For example, you can set up email autoresponders so that people automatically get a monthly newsletter when they sign up. Or you can automate vaccine reminders for your pets.

Partner with Similar Services

There are other businesses within the pet industry that can benefit your clients, such as groomers. When you can connect with your customers, you can increase the chance of finding new clients. Consider partnering with these businesses and cross-promoting.

Expand Services

You may find your clients asking for specific services.

Consider which additional services you can offer with minimal difficulty. You should also consider what has the highest value for your customers.

Expanding offerings can be a great way to keep clients coming back, and this is easier than finding new clients.

MEASURE EVERYTHING

Whether it be marketing, sales or even how many pets you house, you should measure it. This gives you a baseline you can use in the future.

Conclusion

Using the information in this guide will get you started on the right foot toward starting a pet hotel. Your individual business may have unique needs, or you may find that some decisions are not covered here. But as with most pet industry businesses, you can use resilience to find solutions that help your business thrive and grow. This is a new industry poised for significant growth, and now is your chance to get in on the ground floor.

www.ingramcontent.com/pod-product-compliance
Lightning Source LLC
Chambersburg PA
CBHW070623220526
45466CB00001B/81